Praise for Edna A. Castillo
and This Book

"A powerful book to transform your life in wellness and healing. I highly recommend this book."

— Mary Morrissey, Founder of the Brave Thinking Institute

"Edna Castillo reaches out a trustworthy hand and walks beside her readers to remind us of who we are in spiritual truth. She constantly encourages while demonstrating how to move forward by authentically sharing her own life challenges and triumphs. Rich with practical exercises and spiritual guidance, this book can help anyone live their intuitive genius."

— Rev. Kristin Powell, Lead Minister at
Unity of Walnut Creek, California

"The poet Rumi once said, 'Your task is not to seek for love, but merely to seek and find all the barriers within yourself that you have built against it.' In *Living Your Intuitive Genius*, Edna Castillo shares the truths about how she has spent a lifetime removing those barriers to experience the power of forgiveness, heal her body, and connect with her soul. This book will help you remove the barriers standing in your way from living your purpose in fulfilling ways."

— Nicole Gabriel, Author of *Finding Your Inner Truth* and *Stepping Into Your Becoming*

"Edna is one of the most grounded transformational coaches with a niche in wellness that I have ever worked alongside. She not only speaks from a heart-centered curriculum in healing, but she has applied her teachings in her own healing journey. When you work with Edna, you have a sense of her deep cultural connection to nature's pharmacy, combined with her strength in turning 'Adversity into her University.' Her book will undoubtedly take you on a journey of hope beyond the symptom level to the gifts seeking to emerge on your own health journey."

— Karie Cassell, Registered Dietitian, Life Mastery Consultant, and Author of the #1 Bestseller *The Domino Diet*

"Like so many of us, Edna Castillo has had to make difficult decisions, often going against what she was taught was right growing up, but she found that what society or religion taught her was not always the right path for her. In *Living Your Intuitive Genius*, she teaches us how to listen to that inner voice that will guide us to making powerful decisions that will heal our body, mind, and soul. I could relate to so much Edna shared and the tools and exercises she offered were life-changing."

— Tyler R. Tichelaar, PhD and Award-Winning Author of *Narrow Lives* and *The Best Place*

"In *Living Your Intuitive Genius*, Edna Castillo takes us on a journey of letting go and letting God. The intuitive genius she references is that inner wisdom we all get from our Higher Power. She offers simple but powerful exercises to help us listen better so we can empower ourselves to heal and propel our lives forward, making us happier, healthier people and inspirations to others."

— Patrick Snow, Publishing Coach and International Bestselling Author
of *Creating Your Own Destiny* and *The Affluent Entrepreneur*

"Are you aware of the beliefs that are affecting your life today? Are you asking yourself 'Is there more to my life than what I have today?' Edna has outlined in this textbook of living your life fully alive how to move from where you are to a life you would love living. She is a wise woman who has lived and is daily living the connection to her soul. The book contains steps to take to expand your thinking, connect with your Higher Self, and live the life you would love. Your journey starts today with Edna as your guide."

— Carole Ostendorf, PhD in Counseling
Psychology and Life Mastery Consultant

"Edna is living proof that walking in love is the path to a life well lived. No matter the obstacles she's faced in her life, Edna has thrived forward. I love how she has turned her most recent health journey of breast cancer into an opportunity to transcend her life even further. Living Your Intuitive Genius is a must-read book if you're looking to up-level any area of your life, transcend all obstacles, and become your best self!"

— Samantha Kaaua, Bestselling Author, Speaker, Founder, and CEO of The GEMMS, Licensed Marriage & Family Therapist and Relationship Coach

"If you've been struggling with unanswered life questions, this book is for you. Castillo simplifies how to break through limiting beliefs. Instead of dwelling in problems, you can use this amazing book to empower your inner self to lead your mind and physical body toward a satisfying life experience."

— Lucky McCullough, Author of *Quiet Your Mind Chatter*

"I had the honor and privilege to walk alongside Edna during her thriving journey through cancer. As a fellow mindset coach, a friend, and a woman, she amazes me all the time with her grace, wisdom and love. It has been a gift to me to witness her journey. We met on a weekly basis as partners-in-believing throughout her treatment period. Every week Edna shared her new awareness of mindset and wellness that she discovered on her path to health. Now Edna is sharing her beautiful gift with the world to help others who are seeking the true meaning of health. I am so thrilled for her and for what this world is about to receive!"

— Lin Yuan-Su, Success Coach, MScFN, Registered Dietician, Founder and President of Lin Yuan-Su Success Coach Inc.; Co-Owner of Shang Gong Chinese Medicine Wellness Centre, in London, Ontario, Canada

"I highly recommend Edna's Living Your Intuitive Genius. It captures the inspired wisdom she acquired during her own journey with cancer. Edna shares the lessons she learned and encourages us to find our intuitive genius by listening to our inner guidance as we walk the human path. She offers helpful exercises that unveil our truest self—The Healed Self. Beautifully done, Edna! Bravo!"

— R. Consuelo Inez, Intuitive Medicine Woman, Founder and President of Inez Healing Arts

Going from Surviving to Thriving

Living Your Intuitive Genius

How to Tap Into Your Soul to Heal Your Body, Mind, and Spirit

Edna A. Castillo

AVIVA
PUBLISHING
New York

LIVING YOUR INTUITIVE GENIUS
How to Tap Into Your Soul to Heal Your Body, Mind, and Spirit

Published by:
Aviva Publishing
Lake Placid, NY
(518) 523-1320
www.AvivaPubs.com

Address all inquiries to:
Edna A. Castillo
www.LivingRealityDreams.com
edna@livingrealitydreams.com
(925) 202-1042

ISBN: 978-1-63618-209-4 Softcover
        978-1-63618-235-3 Hardcover
Library of Congress Control Number: 2022913973

Editors: Tyler Tichelaar and Larry Alexander, Superior Book Productions
Cover Design: Nicole Gabriel, Angel Dog Productions
Interior Book Layout: Nicole Gabriel, Angel Dog Productions
Author Photo: Emma Aravelo

Every attempt has been made to properly source all quotes.
Printed in the United States of America
First Edition

2 4 6 8 10 12

Dedication

"I love you not because of who you are, but
because of who I am when I am with you."
— Roy Croft

To the Being who breathes life into me. I am grateful for life as it grows me and nurtures me. I am listening.

To my parents, Jacob and Marina Arevalo, who modeled how to go after your dreams by emigrating to the US with a dream for their children to enjoy a better life. Your love and dedication to God and family concretized my values which have served me well.

To my husband, Daniel Castillo, who is my biggest cheerleader and supporter in all I do, create, believe, and embrace. I love you.

To my children, Xochitl and Alex Duenas, who gifted me the honor of being their mama; it's my highest purpose, and I am honored and privileged; you are my teachers. Your love and care mean the world to me.

To my bonus children, Amy, Michael, and Ryan Castillo, whom I love as my own. It's my privilege to be part of your lives. You honor your mom, Ruthi, with the outstanding people you've become.

To my siblings, both biological and in-love (in-laws), whose love and care carried me while I was navigating my health journey and who support my efforts to live my dream. Walking life with you at my side has been a joyous and love filled experience.

To Mary Morrissey, Kirsten Welles, and the Brave Thinking Institute faculty whose teachings carried me during my health journey. This book would not have been possible without you.

To all who are diagnosed and living their health journey by staying in a wellness, healing, and health mindset.

To you, my reader, to whom I wish wellness and health as you discover how to heal your life.

Acknowledgments

I wish to thank the following people who have inspired and supported me in the process of publishing this book:

Larry Alexander	Samantha Kaaua
Marina Arevalo	Mary M. Morrissey
Brave Thinking Institute	Bob Proctor
Karie Cassell	Patrick Snow
Daniel Castillo	Tyler Tichelaar
Nicole Gabriel	Kirsten Welles
Marianne Williamson	Rev. Kristin Powell
A Course in Miracles	Lin Yuan-Su
Tomomi Ito	Regina, my nurse

Contents

A Note to the Reader

"Don't turn away. Keep your gaze on the ban-
daged place. That's where the light enters you."

— Rumi

The inspiration for this book was walking a health journey in which I faced breast cancer. My intent is to share my story without making it about me but about the lessons I learned that contributed to my healing.

If you are currently diagnosed with a medical condition and looking for information that can help now, I invite you to read Chapter 11: Self-Leadership and Chapter 12: The Journey first. These chapters describe how you are born with the genius inside to heal and how I applied the Laws of the Universe to heal from the inside out. Then move forward to the other chapters in the order they are presented.

This book was inspired by Spirit's presence. The events and stories are real, although the names were changed to protect their privacy, and the public figures are named for the contribution they made in my life as my teachers.

I chose this book's title *Living Your Intuitive Genius* because I believe we all have the power inside us to heal ourselves. It is our intuitive genius that gives us the wisdom to create that healing. We just have to listen to it. The subtitle is *How to Tap Into Your Soul to Heal Your Body, Mind, and Spirit*. The mind, body, and soul are the three essential parts of our existence that need to be healthy and in balance for us to live a vibrant life. Your soul is your inner spirit, which can be accessed for the answers and growth you are seeking. The practices in this book will lead you to living a life that is more connected with Spirit or God, the Creator of all beings, and thereby opening yourself to living a fuller, more expansive, abundant life.

As you read the book, keep in mind we are all on this human journey with our own level of awareness; therefore, the information may be new or out of your realm. I encourage you to keep an open mind to the possibilities for learning something new. When I read *The Power of Now* by Eckhart Tolle for the first time, I simply did not understand what he wrote. When I picked up the same book years later, it all fell into place for me. Likewise, as you read you may ask, "What in the world is she talking about? That just can't be so." If you perceive the points or conclusions I make differently, I invite you to share your thoughts with me. This book is our book, and we can learn from each other. You will find my contact information in the back of the book. I look forward to hearing your feedback so I can revise the concepts to enrich us all.

Let's face it; we are all on a healing journey. Mine was a breast cancer journey. Your healing may be from a betrayal, a loss, or devastating financial conditions; whatever the situation, you are invited to make peace with that journey and move on with the power of healing. You heal as you accept the situation as a gift you are given to grow into your new becoming. It is with the grace of God (Source, Infinite Intelligence, your Higher Power) that we make this trek and polish ourselves into a shining gem by living through the tough circumstances we face. One of my favorite spiritual teachers, Ram Dass, said, "Healing does not mean going back to the way things were before, but rather allowing what is now to move us closer to God."

If you are asking *why* you are living with a health condition, I say let go of the why, and at the same time, ask your Source to send you the answer. We don't have to find the why—the mystery is part of the gift—but in some cases, the answer may be helpful. This is what happened to me. I understood how powerful my thoughts are; the breast cancer diagnosis was evidence of the power of my mind. And it has now allowed me to experiment more with other aspects of my thoughts. Keeping my thoughts reined in and trusting the process of life has become my primary mode of operation. Trusting the process is rigorous work, and at times, when I choose to be lax with some of the practices, I am quickly reminded that if I want results, I have to do the work—starting with my thoughts. Your answers will come in accordance with how they are to serve you as you move forward.

This book, with its ideas, information, strategies, exercises, and wisdom, is my offering to all seeking to heal a part of themselves that is keeping them from becoming whom they would love to be. It is a discovery I made during this spiritual journey. It all came together when I faced the most challenging health journey. Without health, we have nothing, so when our health suffers, our entire life is altered as we navigate that time. And while I was writing this book, I had many enlightening moments in which I learned even more, as Spirit was working within me to birth *Living Your Intuitive Genius*. The title came from Spirit. One of my strongest nudges was to continue writing until I felt empty and could write no more.

You are invited to engage in the chapter exercises. They work; they helped me develop as a person. Continuing the practices for an extended time will create change.

Part of our human journey is to learn not to resist change. When we resist, it causes friction and delays our lessons, so as we dive into this work, we are in essence telling our subconscious we are ready to evolve into our new self. In resistance we find more pain and suffering, so leaving victimhood behind and knowing that suffering is a choice is the first step to transforming our lives.

Are you ready to transform? Are you ready to heal? Are you ready to live in peace, love, and harmony? I offer congratulations on your courage and willingness to look at life as a friend who welcomes you into becoming you.

Introduction

Collecting the Nuggets

"Enlightenment is always preceded by confusion."

— Milton H. Erickson

hy me? There must be a mistake. What did I do to deserve this? This is not happening to me. These are the thoughts that run through your mind after being diagnosed with a life-threatening illness. Whatever health journey you are facing, questioning it is normal. You always think such illnesses happen to other people, so when you are the one affected, it is difficult to come to grips with reality.

Unless the illness was passed down through your family, or you are aware of your thinking, you may never know why you were chosen for this struggle. The question is whether you will remain stuck in the question or move forward deciding to collect as many nuggets of wisdom as you can from this experience you are being gifted.

Every journey has a purpose. Have you seen a trend in your life? You have encountered other difficult challenges before; perhaps you've been through a divorce, a financial crisis, a heartbreak, or academic or career trials. As you reflect on your life's tapestry, you may realize the situations you least preferred were the ones that brought the most growth. Even though you did not want it, you did not ask for it, and you rejected it, the journey you are on may be the one you are now the proudest of. And here you are again, facing a new one.

The way you navigate this journey will speak to how you will continue to navigate your life; you can't afford to get stuck. This journey could take your life, or it could become a lifelong journey that never goes away—one that will forever haunt you because even if you defeat it, you may fear it will come back. This is when the way you represent yourself or "show up" matters most—showing up as a victim or victor may determine the outcome of your life.

In this book, you will learn how letting go of the *why* and embracing the *what* is key to minimizing the effects of the disease or whatever difficulties you face. It is important to remain faithful to the process and the belief that this difficulty is here to give you the gift of awareness about things you previously ignored. You ignored the beauty of life, the laws present in your life's journey, the powers you innately hold yet do not use, and the genius that exists within your body and mind. You are now awakened and will discover a different way to perceive life and live it. You will discover your oneness with all living things and make welcome the growth and nuggets of wisdom the journey gives you.

As you apply the wisdom, knowledge, experience, skills, strategies, and techniques offered in this book, you will learn how to tap into your soul to heal your body, mind, and spirit. The practices herein are a way of life, and as you welcome them, you will receive a most wonderful gift—the awareness that everything you need is inside of you; the choice to move forward living your life by listening to the genius within is yours.

The most important wisdom you can take away from this book is that life is a gift, and deciding to treat life as a gift will provide a new level of understanding. You will become aware that you are life, you are the creator of your life, and your results reflect your thoughts, feelings, and actions. When challenges arise, it is because life sees the opportunity for emerging awareness to expand within you—to expand your abilities. Think about one of the challenges you've already overcome. Can you see the growth that occurred within you as a result? A new you emerged. That journey began with an undesired condition that did not feel good, but the gift you received from it is one you would not give back.

I believe you are no different than I am, and you may have or will come up with a similar realization about life to my own. I was born with a curiosity that made me question what life was about, and the more I stayed in that question, the more I received answers. I see other people on their own paths of discovery; many of them I can learn from, including you. I believe we are here to serve one another in any way we can. We lift each other up as we move through life. During my health journey, I have seen people who may benefit from knowing what I have learned. Life continues to gift me with more experiences, and up until now, the breast cancer journey has been one I would not want anyone to undergo, yet everyone should have the gift it gave me. That is the reason for this book—to share my experience so it might help anyone traversing an illness or a challenging event or circumstance.

Perhaps my curiosity is what has led me to so many well-lived experiences. I came to a new country as an immigrant and assimilated with the culture in the United States so well it directly conflicted with the values, beliefs, and reality I knew in Guatemala. I excelled as a student but did not fulfill my dream of graduating from an Ivy League school. I was a devout Catholic whose divorce journey was long, arduous, and painful. I was a single parent for ten-plus years before I met my new husband, Daniel, who values me as an equal partner. I had great career opportunities and financial success, yet I lost my home and had to start all over during the financial crisis of 2008-2009, and then I reached a point where everything was going wonderfully, only to face a breast cancer journey and discover a holy individual relationship with God. This roller coaster of experiences prepared me for becoming a life coach; after all, how can you walk with someone in their life journey if you have no reference for what they are experiencing? I love my life, and I love the journey because of all the nuggets of wisdom I've received along the way can help others on their journeys. The beauty is that the journey and learning will continue until the last breath I will be gifted to enjoy.

I know you are on your own journey. The tapestry of your life is in the making, and the day-in-and-day-out circumstances you face make it difficult to pursue all your dreams, goals, and visions. You may be a single parent, working multiple jobs to make ends meet, or the breadwinner of your family, but now you face a health event that seems insurmountable, or you may be undergoing your own divorce; you are experiencing your toughest journey thus far. And in those moments, the pursuit of your dream is clouded by the conditions outside of you. But remember, overcoming obstacles is part of our human journey.

I believe in you.

I am with you.

I am you.

I know your possibilities are even more than you can envision. I believe God has a sense of humor because when our dreams come true, they are bigger than we ever imagined. And I know you have all it takes to make your reality reflect your dreams.

When you picked up this book, part of you was ready to begin a transformational journey. The part of you that relates to Source and listens to the little voice within—that part of you that knows you are here to leave a footprint on humanity and your dreams are your gift for the world —is ready to begin the next leg of the journey. Are you ready to get started? And are you willing to go to any length to change your results? If the answer is yes, are you willing to trust the process? The process is life; trust that your journey is here to give you the perfect gift, the one you are here to receive. Life is perfection, and to achieve its perfection, it works in the chaos we feel in our lives. Trust that you are always given the answers, and you are supported every step of the way.

Let's begin! You are the ruler of your life; this is your time, and your willingness will give you the energy you need to succeed.

Chapter 1

Recognizing the Power Within

"What lies behind us and what lies ahead of us are tiny matters
compared to what lives within us."
— Henry David Thoreau

A s you start your transformational journey, it is important to set
your intention. I recommend that intention be to embrace the
true transformation that will result and the person you will become,
the person you are meant to be and who already exists in the eye of
the Infinite Intelligence, the One Source that knows all and gives all.
(Refer to the exercise on setting intention at the end of this chapter.)

On this journey, you are the ruler of your life; you are the highest
authority of who you are and who you are to become. Embracing the
journey with gratitude for the good and the golden nuggets picked
up along the way will feed your journey with more wisdom, more
love, and more joy.

Setting an intention calls for opening your heart to be loved, to be squeezed, to be tugged, to be made uncomfortable, and to welcome everything, knowing it is perfection. Setting intention is holding the vision of who you see yourself being—for example, someone who can dance or sing in front of others without caring what they say or think—and acting freely as you are meant to do. Don't hold back. Let yourself be all in. The intention will set the energy flowing into and creating the new you, the you whom you've always known and seen, the you who speaks to your heart and has no doubt you are a genuine being living within your power as supported by God.

You have the power within. You were born with special gifts unique to you, and you are here to live a unique purpose. Within you lies the answer to your magical gift, yet when you've tried to find it in the past, it has evaded you. You can find your gifts using a logic-based method like taking personality tests. They can reveal your strengths, yet they do not reveal your true purpose. The answers you seek come from within. Your inner wisdom speaks to you to lead you to understanding the inner you and who you are meant to be.

You may be in a job that pays the bills, and you may even enjoy it, yet in your heart you feel there is more. You long for more. You have a void within that longs to be filled and honored, but your fears and self-limiting beliefs keep you from exploring and listening to the inner voice.

The biggest obstacle to discovery may be what others say or expect of you—your responsibilities to others. If you are a parent, you may feel seeking your passion is irresponsible or it is too late for you to pursue it. It is never too late. In fact, all things that come to us come at exactly the right time.

The longing you feel today is related to yesterday's experiences. You have been serving your purpose, and now the journey calls you to move forward to discover more about you. Your inner wisdom— your spirit—is asking you to grow upward like the spiral of your DNA. Every living organism is asked to do this; every flower and animal is called to become what they are to be. An oak tree follows the same process life is calling you to honor. Do not fear the journey ahead. Do not try to ignore it. It will continue to nudge you, and with the wisdom of the Infinite Intelligence, the nudges will get louder. The journey can be painful when you do not listen. Life becomes more difficult and circumstances yell at you to change direction and discover and honor your becoming.

The Loud, Resounding Voice

The nudges, the situations, and the coincidences will continue lining up until you act. Life may start taking on the tone of stuck energy where you become physically sick or experience conflict in your relationships. Life will continue to become more complex until you listen to the voice within. If you do not heed the voice, it will become very loud.

I worked in a corporate financial services environment for thirty years before Infinite Intelligence gave me a clear signal that it was time for a career change. I had climbed the corporate ladder and enjoyed my work, which I was exceptionally good at. I was still engaged, yet a voice inside said, "There has to be more than this." When I left the office at night, I could feel I wasn't doing what I was meant to do. I knew my purpose was bigger than adding zeros to the bottom line of a multinational corporation.

In hindsight, the signals were loud and clear, but I was not tuned into the message. I did not have the tools to receive the information and act on what Life was telling me. I was still focused on financial gain, being seen as responsible, and providing for my family, even though I felt an inner emptiness.

I had been walking this path for thirty years.

The nudge to change became overwhelming when my work circumstances changed, and I was no longer reporting to a strong leader. In hindsight, I see Life was speaking loudly, telling me to honor myself, move on, find happiness, find joy, and align once again with health. In the moment, I had failed to rise above the surface and see the situation for what it was—the screaming voice of discontent. When you listen to your inner voice, you have the power to propel change. Your inner voice can clearly tell you if you are moving with or against the flow of life. When you experience things not working and you push for things to happen your way, you are failing to understand that controlling a situation is a way of moving against the flow of life rather than with it.

Since I did not listen to life's signals and initiate the change it was calling me to make, Life forced me to look at the alternatives for serving Life moving forward by removing me from that job—I was laid off when the company moved to another state. This experience demonstrated how people and events on the road ahead will help you examine your purpose and seek power from within to be, have, create, do, and give anything you want. Know that in those decisions, you are supported.

Listening to Life's Signals

I've seen plenty of evidence of life supporting your actions when you've chosen the life-giving path. One personal event that stands out came soon after my divorce. My divorce was painful because the paradigm of a happily-ever-after marriage was part of my beliefs. My Catholic upbringing fed the shame, fear, regret, blame, and other discouraging feelings I had around divorce, even though it was exactly what Life was nudging me to do to grow. My marriage was suffocating my creativity, love for life, and self-love, belief, and self-care.

That divorce was the right decision became obvious in my and my husband's friendly ending and support for one another; we had no bitterness, hate, or long, drawn-out legal battle. We simply completed a form, divided our stuff, and filed the form with the court. Six months later, the divorce was official. I hurt because I blamed myself for breaking my promise to God and being unable to make a forever home. It is interesting how we tell ourselves stories and believe them although the facts do not support those claims. That is what I did, and it was the reason for my misery for five years after the divorce. The voice in my head told me I was a victim, a failure, a sinner. And all along, Life was supporting my decision and showing me how to proceed—if I would just see the signs. There were three of them.

Sign number one: After the divorce, I moved in with my parents. Within a few months, a good friend asked if I wanted to rent his condominium because he was moving. He would rent it to me at cost; I just needed to pay the mortgage and association fees. God opened the door for me to live in a very safe place without the hassle of finding and qualifying to rent a place. The price was right, too. It was exactly what I could afford.

Sign number two: A few months later, I was promoted and given a raise that tripled my income. I had not asked for the promotion. In fact, I did not have the self-image to see myself fulfilling the new role. Being a supervisor never occurred to me. Since childhood, I had built for myself the paradigm that I was less than others, especially men. As a young girl, I had begun to fight against this paradigm, but then I had married into the same skewed beliefs that proposed women were a grade lower than men. That paradigm was ingrained in me from childhood and reinforced in my marriage.

Sign number three: While divorced, living as a single mom, and maintaining a friendship with my ex-husband, part of me continued to hold on to "the idea" of my marriage. I did not want to let go and would imagine how we could "make it work," even though he was dating and had moved on. During this time, I experienced three car accidents. I was rear-ended each time; each accident occurred within six weeks of another, and in all instances, I was hit by a white car or truck. Two of the accidents resulted in my car being totaled, yet I was not injured. When the last accident happened, a friend's mother asked what might be behind such a streak—what was I doing or thinking to manifest this in my life?

At the time, I had no idea what my friend's mom was suggesting, but I listened and became curious. She asked me what I was doing or thinking when the accidents happened. I saw each accident had a common theme; I had been looking in the rearview mirror or looking at myself in the visor mirror. Her interpretation of my actions was that I was looking backward. She said I was hanging on to something in my past, and the Universe was telling me to move forward and let go.

At the time, I did not fully embrace the wisdom of her words, but I did start trying to move on. I had no more accidents after that—just the pain of letting go, working on myself, and starting anew. This was the first time I understood Life gives us signs; we just have to be awake and willing to listen.

American entrepreneur and visionary Steve Jobs said, "You can't connect the dots looking forward; you can only connect them looking backwards." By connecting the dots, I saw how Life was supporting and reassuring me that the divorce was the right course: a home became available without me searching; my finances became easier to manage; when I was not willing to let go, three nudges disguised as accidents came along to move me forward; and the wisdom of a friend's mother helped me interpret what Life was telling me.

You have the power within to navigate life, knowing you have all the resources you need to do, have, create, give, and be whatever you dream. The dream in your heart would not exist if it were not possible. That thought about what you want, your dream, is Spirit talking and planting the seed of what is possible. It is up to you to make it a reality by believing in yourself and in God, the infinite provider of all.

Listen for the longing and discontent in your life and follow your dreams. You will discover all it really takes is having the trust to take the steps needed to bring your dreams to life.

Exercise A

Knowing that we are fully supported in our life journey opens the door to learning how to communicate with God. Working with the power of Intention connects us to Source and helps us manifest our desires. Intention is a way of communicating what we seek in the end and drawing the energy of God to assist in the process. Using this practice to generate measurable results, we develop the confidence and trust to move forward toward our dreams.

Use this practice as you start each day, setting the intention of how you would like the day to be. See yourself in the energy you would enjoy conveying throughout the day. If you know what you want to obtain, then see yourself doing so. If you have an important meeting, define the outcome you want. Set an intention that would result in a win-win for all involved.

1. Breathe in deeply through your nose; then exhale slowly through your mouth at a slow, comfortable pace. Breathe comfortably this way until you feel relaxed.

2. While you are breathing, bring the outcome you are looking for into your imagination.

3. If possible, state out loud the outcome you are looking for as an affirmation.

4. Feel and imagine what it will look like when it all works out. How would you feel? Be grateful for it all working out as you expected.

5. Feel the energy in your body elevate and vibrate higher and remember that feeling.

6. As you remember throughout the day, think back to the energy; set yourself in that energy as often as you can.

Several things are at play when doing this intention practice. You are breathing to change the vibration in your body to a state of rest, digest, and create. You are imagining the result as if you are watching a movie in your head— producing the results in your mind is the best demonstration of what you would like. If you can verbally communicate the result, it adds to the vibration of the energy you are producing so you are using as many of your senses as possible. You can write your intention and use all your senses to activate the feeling of being there and experiencing the event. Making the result as real as possible in your mind and consciousness provides a clear image of the intention and the outcome you seek. By watching yourself receive exactly what you imagine, you raise your vibration because you are instantly grateful. Staying in gratitude as long as you can places you at a higher vibration frequency, which expands your energy to where you think, *I love my life.*

Cultivating an intention practice will affect your life greatly because what you are doing, in essence, is living from a place of abundance and expectation, knowing you are in the right place, doing exactly what you are meant to do, and all that life brings is for your highest good. Life is a mirror of your thoughts, feelings, and emotions. Placing an intention, then putting the attention on your expected result is like speaking to Life, asking it to provide the result you seek. "What you pay attention to grows," Deepak Chopra said. Simply put, the energy of your thoughts flowing toward a result will likely generate the result you are seeking.

Exercise B

I encourage you to take notes on your intention setting and the results you receive in the space below. Recording your experience and successes will expand your ability to use the power of intention diligently. The more you record, the more evidence you have that the practice works, and the more you will practice it. Recording your wins also serves to raise your vibration when you find you may not be having the success you seek. Since what you pay attention to grows, by recording the successes, you are expanding your field to be able to receive more.

To get started, try a fun intention like finding a parking spot, getting all green lights, or getting the answers you are looking for to a specific thing by a certain day.

_____

_____

_____

_____

Summary

Thirteenth-century Persian poet Rumi said, "Stop acting so small; you are the universe in ecstatic motion." This quote awakens you to realizing you are greater than you know. You are capable of so much more than what you thought or have accomplished so far. It tells you to find the freedom to be the you that you imagined all along and to keep the possibilities of what you may not yet have thought was within you alive. You have the power of God supporting you; you will see the doors and coincidences once you take the steps to flow with Life. When you listen to your inner wisdom, you will experience the still small voice or gut feeling within that represents the real power of who you are. Like Eckhart Tolle said, "Life is the dancer; you are the dance." You will experience life living through you. You will see the world differently and expect and receive from Life only the good.

Chapter 2

Being Courageous

"Whatever you do, you need courage. Whatever course you decide upon, there is always someone to tell you that you are wrong. There are always difficulties arising that tempt you to believe your critics are right. To map out a course of action and follow it to an end requires some of the same courage that a soldier needs."

— Ralph Waldo Emerson

In the last chapter, you discovered you have the power within to have, create, give, and be anything you wish. You are a creative source. You can create your own reality and outperform your own self-image once you trust, believe, and expect to receive. The issue may be you grew up in paradigms that led you to believe you did not deserve what you want. Your subconscious mind does not believe you are worthy. Then the self-talk against your desires starts, and you start talking yourself out of what you want. You start saying you are not good enough or deserving enough. You begin to doubt why you would ever do, have, or create what your heart desires.

But you are here on earth to do exactly that. And to ease your journey, your superpower is courage.

Courage is defined as the ability to do something that frightens us, or having strength in the face of pain or grief. It's easy to think of courageous people as those who have done or are doing extraordinary things, but you are courageous when you face small fears in the same way you face life-threatening circumstances. The recipe for courage is the same. Courage lies in the actions you take when you dare to be you.

It takes courage to be you, to stand for what you believe in, to believe in yourself despite what others think or say, to continue to act despite the circumstances, to show up for yourself no matter what. You may think that courage is part of heroism, valor, fearlessness, and greatness, but courage is mostly displayed in your everyday life.

Up until now, you have become aware of fears that have become part of who you are as you grew up. When your parents showed you their fears, they may have become your own. Fears were instilled in you as you experienced the world, and since each person has different experiences, your fears are unique to you.

Your fears or paradigms can hold you back from becoming whom you would love to be or stop you from creating the life you would love to create. You were born with many gifts, and you grew into your fears based on your experiences and what you've been told is possible for you. Courage is facing your fears, uncovering your paradigms, and looking them squarely in the eye and overcoming them by action. The action of courage is simply being you. You have a unique value system; courage is developed as you stand for your values and uniqueness without reservation.

Being courageous is not easy. You face many barriers, starting with your thoughts and feelings. What do your thoughts say when you are facing your fears? Likely your thoughts are creating doubt and obstacles to moving forward. Your self-talk is saying you are acting in vain and is questioning why you put so much energy into this one thing. What makes you think it's possible when you have not succeeded in the past? You don't have it in you to succeed. The odds are against you. Why now? Why not wait until a better time when the circumstances change? Your thoughts are in the habit of protecting you, of softening your fall, and keeping you safe from failure. The self-talk has had years to perfect itself and know exactly what to say to dissuade, distract, or delay; therefore, changing a belief system to live a life of courage is a rigorous process.

A life of courage consists of small acts taken despite the lack of evidence to support them, acts that, deep inside, you know are right actions. Steps of courage are the steppingstones that pave a path to your Becoming, as you trust you are doing the right thing in the interest of growth. You follow your instinct despite the self-talk and inner critic that fights to keep you comfortable.

We witness acts of courage all the time, and at times, we question if we would have been able to act as bravely when presented with the actions of others we admire. We see courageous people honored in our history books, so we often don't see our actions as courageous by comparison. How can you, asking a question at a meeting, compare to the actions of someone like Rosa Parks, who refused to give up her seat on the bus as dictated by segregation? How can you compare the courage of an immigrant with fifty dollars in their pocket who traveled across oceans and left comfort behind to you acting by asking that special person out on a first date? There is no need to compare. They are all courageous actions; they are decisions made hesitantly, with fear or doubt about the outcome. Courage is courage. Society may label some acts as grand and not others, but it is still the same courage.

William H. Murray's Question

William Hutchinson Murray, the author of *Evidence of Things Not Seen*, is credited with saying:

Until one is committed, there is hesitancy, the chance to draw back, always ineffectiveness. Concerning all acts of initiative and creation, there is one elementary truth, the ignorance of which kills countless ideas and splendid plans. It is this: The moment one definitely commits oneself, then providence moves you. All sorts of things occur to help one that would never otherwise have occurred. A whole stream of events issue from the decision, raising in one's favor all manner of unforeseen incidents and meetings and material assistance, which no man or woman could have dreamed would have come his/her way.

Murray was a Scottish mountaineer who was invited by Sir Edmund Hillary to climb Mount Everest. As a climber, he had to pay his own way. Murray was asked by Hillary several times whenever Hillary was planning a new expedition. The first two times, Murray asked how much it would cost, and each time, he decided he could not afford it. The last time, Murray asked a different question, which led to him joining the famous expedition up the South Col of Everest, which discovered the route that led to the first successful summiting of the peak. The question this time was, "How much is the down payment?" He knew that if not now, then his chance at summiting Everest might never come, and that once he decided, God would work in his favor to make it possible. He had faith that Providence would make it possible.

Led to Courage

W. H. Murray, Rosa Parks, you, and me have episodes of courage. Deciding to leave my marriage was an act of courage. It was a normal day, with nothing extraordinary going on, although the week had been full of emotion and disappointment. My life was not what I had imagined. I had always imagined marriage as a supportive relationship between equals who cheered and lifted each other up. I married someone whose upbring encouraged traditional gender roles and who perceived my desire to grow as a threat to his masculine pride. I ached to be validated and loved.

In the web of thoughts and feelings about my situation, I was confused and lacked confidence. My body was not even mine since I had gained about fifty pounds dealing with my feelings. I was trapped by my religious upbringing, which dictated "until death do us part." No part of me saw the end of my marriage until that day.

Today, I question whether I would have come to that decision if I had not stopped to buy gas on my way home from work. As I was pumping gas, I saw a little girl in the backseat of the car on the other side of the pumps. Her eyes met mine; my body froze in time for a few seconds, and then I knew. There was no other answer. I must get a divorce. In those few seconds, my thoughts went to my daughter—the same age as the little girl in the car. My thoughts went to a few years from then when my daughter could better comprehend or feel my experience. My daughter couldn't grow up seeing me this way, couldn't grow up thinking that our marriage reflected a "normal" relationship between a husband and wife. Up until then, because she was young, my daughter had not seen me crying, my insecurities, or my experience, and since she had not witnessed any of that, it was not too late to show her a different way of living—show her a life where women are respected, honored, loved, supported, and appreciated, and to show her a mom who loves herself and walks with confidence. I wanted to make my daughter proud.

In that moment, I was led to courage. I had no intention of becoming a single mother, but events led me to feel the exhaustion of being me, of living a life where I felt numb. The courage to divorce my husband came from my love for my daughter. My love for her saved my life.

The decision to divorce was a single step followed by hundreds of other actions culminating in discovering myself again.

Your steps in courage may be prompted by pain, circumstance, or love for another person. The important thing is to act once you make the decision. Act knowing there is a supportive, loving God cheering for your success. The voice in your head will work to keep you where you are through fear, doubt, and worry about what will be. But you do not have to listen to it.

Affirmations are a tool that helps you rewrite the statements coming from the voice in your head. They are statements that offer emotional support and encouragement. When repeated, they help rewrite the negative thoughts or statements of your self-talk. They are also known as "I am" statements and are believed to have the highest energy vibration because they provide a direct connection to God.

I Am That I Am

God said to Moses, "I AM WHO I AM." And he said, "Say this to the people of Israel: 'I AM has sent me to you.'"

— Exodus 3:14

According to the Christian faith, I AM is God's name. It is more than a name; it has immense power, and it is a statement of God's being. Making "I am" statements part of your practice is affirming God is within you. The statement "I am" in essence means "I am one with God." This is the most powerful statement you can ever make because it has the power of God within it. We are spiritual beings living in a spiritual universe; therefore, the statement reinforces our belief that the power of the universe is behind us, supporting us, and manifesting our desires.

Since "I am" is such a powerful statement, by repeating it, you over-write your subconscious belief system, in essence reprograming your brain to remove limiting beliefs and the thoughts behind them and replacing them with a belief in empowering thoughts. Concentrating on expanded thoughts, instead of constricting thoughts, will help change the pattern of your thoughts, beliefs, and feelings. The reticular activating system of your brain filters in the new thought patterns and you start thinking more of those thoughts, believing in them, and generating positive, uplifting emotions that lead to feeling better. Similarly, as with the Intention exercise, the more sensory channels you engage, the stronger the energy signal you generate. Some people journal or write the affirmations, others recite them, and others read them.

When I was coming out of the divorce, my self-esteem and self-worth were extremely low; I was overweight and felt ugly, fat, short, dumb, and many more adjectives that played in my head as negative beliefs about who I was. But inside that person was the real me—the beautiful young woman with a positive impression of herself who knew she could do anything. I did not believe in me after the divorce, but I knew the belief was acquired during the non-nurturing relationship.

My intention was to change the dialogue in my head that made me feel worthless, and the easiest way to change it was to reaffirm my beauty and boost my self-esteem. My partner had not told me in years how beautiful I was, so that affirmation made sense for my state.

My daughter jokes with me now about seeing me singing to myself in the morning while looking in the mirror. Yes, as silly as it sounds, I would sing, "I am beautiful…I'm so beautiful" to myself while getting ready for the day. I knew I needed to turn things around in my mind to begin healing, and regardless of how I felt about doing it, I would still do it daily.

My practice was to sing affirmations as part of my morning routine. This practice continues, although the statements change to address other paradigms I've discovered along the way. I have found singing fun and motivating. It uplifts me in every way. Singing leads to dancing, which itself raises my vibration (and yours). In singing and dancing affirmations, you use your entire body to generate the feelings that will nurture you during the day.

Similarly, with the practice of setting intentions, the more senses you use, the higher the vibration you will have along with better outcomes.

I Am Affirmations

With affirmations, I recommend choosing one or two areas to work on. For example, if you are coming out of a relationship that tore down your self-esteem, then use a few affirmations that will counter those thoughts and feelings. If you are experiencing poor health, concentrate on affirmations that will boost your immune system. The affirmations need to be consistent and available throughout the day or night as you notice negative thoughts.

You may want to develop rituals, such as affirming your beauty, worthiness, and confidence while you are putting on your makeup (or shaving if you're a guy), or affirming vibrant dynamic health while you are showering. You can also use the same affirmation as you are washing dishes, waiting at a stoplight, in line at the grocery store—the point is to have the affirmations available as needed throughout your day. As you do, you overwrite the beliefs rooted in your subconscious.

Being Effective

The interesting thing about affirmations is how simple and powerful they are. I have seen people change their lives by the faithful practice of affirmations. My friend Jane suffers from a challenging condition. When I first met her, it was difficult to have a conversation with her because her speech was slow, disrupted with pauses between syllables, and at times, slurred. It was difficult for Jane to have fluid conversations. When I engaged her in conversation, I had to pay close attention and at times piece phrases together to understand her.

Jane also suffered from other ailments that kept her from enjoying her daily life. Jane was committed to changing the way she was feeling and living. Among her self-treatments, she decided to practice daily affirmations. Her goal was to recite her affirmation at least twenty-five times per day, so she built a prompt into her daily habits to remember and mentally recite the affirmation. The goal was also to say it out loud when possible. In addition, she decided if for some reason she did not meet her twenty-five-times-per-day goal, she would recite the affirmation the remaining times before she went to sleep.

Her affirmation was, "I am enjoying vibrant, dynamic health with every cell in my body working for my highest good."

This is how her practice began; what I witnessed after was remarkable. Our conversations became noticeably smoother. I noticed it was easier to understand her since there were fewer gaps in her speech and I understood more of the conversation. Our conversations became smoother and more fluid. Her illness was not gone, but in just a few months, I saw a noticeable difference. The biggest difference was in her attitude. Because she struggled less to communicate, she felt better. Jane still has health issues, but her demeanor is a lot more positive and the improvements have given her the courage to do more.

Affirmations work. Science shows the mind can be reprogrammed to displace negative thoughts and beliefs. Repeating the thoughts or beliefs you are adopting over time cements them in your subconscious so you start believing them. Ninety-five percent of your thoughts and behaviors originate in your subconscious, where your limiting beliefs, emotional reactions, habits, and conditioned responses lie. To create lasting change in the deep-rooted beliefs that interfere with the image of who you would love to be, you must work on your subconscious mind.

As you practice affirmations, at first you will not believe the statements; then over time, you will start thinking they are possible, and eventually, you will believe. For example, if you doubt your ability to succeed, you can say, "I can succeed. I am successful. I do succeed," as your affirmation. Your repeated use of the statement over a month or months will eventually cause you to believe in your success. You will surprise yourself and feel a shift in your approach to situations that will lead to success. I practiced this mantra over a month and repeated the affirmation during the day, prior to going to sleep, and anytime I woke up in the middle of the night. About twenty days into the practice, I noticed a shift in my energy and the way I felt about succeeding.

It takes commitment to maintain this practice, but it is a simple one you can use to change your life. Commit to repeating affirmations until your belief changes. Once you see the results of this practice—see its power—you will continue to do it, coming back to it over and over as you choose to transform areas of your life and live courageously.

You may have to come back to repattern certain behaviors or thoughts. Neuroscience demonstrates the rewiring that happens and that resets thought and belief patterns. I have seen affirmations work in my life and in others' lives.

Sample Affirmations

I am worthy of my dreams.

I am enough and deserving of _____ [fill in the blank].

I am beautiful, joyful, and confident.

I am loved, loving, lovable.

Every day, in every way, I am getting better and better.

I am enjoying vibrant, energetic, dynamically great health.

I am deeply fulfilled by what I do, say, and create.

I am in a loving and caring relationship.

I am the best [blank] in the world.

I am wealthy and healthy in every area of my life.

I am full of vitality, and my mind is calm and peaceful.

I am open to receiving all the wealth life offers me.

I am worthy of making more money.

I am healthy.

Exercise

In the space provided, identify affirmations that will serve you in living a more courageous, freeing life.

1. Imagine the person you would love to be. Look at yourself as a third party observing yourself living the life you would love to live. Notice what you are noticing about the behaviors and beliefs that serve the vision of the new you. What behaviors do

you see you doing as part of the new you? This is the self-image you are identifying as the new you. Memorize this self-image because you will refer to this person as part of your exercise.

_____

_____

_____

_____

_____

_____

_____

2. Identify current beliefs and thinking patterns keeping you from being that person. Examine your self-talk, feelings, emotions, and beliefs to identify which require repatterning. Look at all the areas where you may have convinced yourself you are less than or not good enough. Write common thoughts you have about yourself now that are keeping you from the person you would love to be.

_____

_____

_____

_____

_____

_____

_____

3. For every limiting behavior or thought you wrote down, think of the opposite thought, feeling, or belief, and come up with an I am affirmation to counter the current paradigm.

_____

_____

_____

_____

_____

_____

_____

4. Write the affirmations on cards or Post-it notes to place where you need reminders of the affirmation. Common places are your bathroom mirror, your refrigerator, your desk, your nightstand,

your journal or Day-Timer, and your car. Place these notes where you can access them throughout the day.

_____

_____

_____

_____

_____

_____

_____

5. Commit to repeating the affirmations several times per day. As you repeat them, remember the person in your future self-image you are holding in your mind as the new you. The more you recite them, the more repatterning you are doing.

After a month or more of affirmation practice, revisit your notes and your thinking to see how your thinking has changed. The greater your commitment, the greater the change; you will discover you believe your new thoughts and your world is open to the new possibilities. You will eventually discover you have internalized this new self-image and become the new you.

Summary

Courage in our daily lives is different for everyone depending on the paradigms and self-talk each person faces. What may be courageous for some may not require any courage for others. Each person faces unique challenges requiring different doses of courage. Each person is called to nurture and practice courage daily. We all face daily challenges that require courage. Whether it's the courage to get up in the morning after a loss or an illness, talking to someone you would love to meet, standing up against an injustice, or deciding to act, they all lead to growth.

When you ignore the thing calling you to change because you lack the courage, your journey stagnates. You were born to grow and flourish, not to sit comfortably stagnating as a person. Stagnation leads to unhappiness, which can lead to mental and bodily illnesses.

Humans are meant to grow in life's journey, and courage supports the decisions and actions you take while on this journey. Courage is a superpower that helps you see who you are meant to be. Courage is a bridge we do not enjoy crossing, yet we celebrate once we have reached the other side. Life is meant to be lived walking hand-in-hand with courage along the way.

Chapter 3

Deciding to Grow

"It takes courage to grow up and become who you really are."

— E. E. Cummings

A merican poet E.E. Cummings said it takes courage to grow up and become who you really are. It also takes courage to decide and set the intention to grow as a person and do the work to live your purpose. My teacher and mentor, Mary Morrisey, said, "The content of our lives is the curriculum of our evolution." I love this statement because it really speaks to why we are here, why we are alive, and what our mission is on our human journey. It calls us to go beyond our current self and grow. We are here to evolve into a better version of who we are. We keep moving up the spiral of our human journey to our becoming—our human journey is about growth.

Your willingness to grow and learn from the curriculum of life defines your journey in the evolution of how you perceive life, in your relationship with life. Some may see themselves as victims of circumstances; when they face difficult times, their first thought may be "Why me? Not again. Can't I catch a break?" This point of view leads to looking outward for answers that are within; therefore, it leads to a life of suffering. This thought process may have been hardwired during childhood, a habit taught by others.

As a group, humans bond by sharing adversity. But this natural instinct to share our hardships, or just crappy days, sends out a negative vibration that is amplified and intensified through repetition. To grow, we must put aside instinct and focus on the happy moments; we must spread that vibration and help it grow.

Understanding you control how much you suffer in any situation, no matter how bad, is an important part of your growth journey. You are not stuck unless you choose to be. You have the capacity to detach yourself from the emotions of suffering like anger, jealousy, frustration, depression, etc. Feeling those emotions is part of the human journey, and controlling them is often difficult. You may be struggling with an internal fight in which part of you would like to stop suffering and the other part is used to the script and finds comfort in suffering.

It is good to honor your feelings, allow yourself to feel your emotions, and at the same time, choose the reactions you will display when they rise inside of you. Understand that only part of you feels this way, and you control your actions. Know that you are in control of your emotions and the suffering you decide to dwell in.

Notice your behaviors and actions to discover whether you are addicted to the drama of suffering. Are you willing to change and live a more peaceful, creative life? Does others' suffering create excitement and drama you may be addicted to? Deciding to grow leads to examining your thoughts, emotions, and reactions so you can make changes leading to a more peaceful and joyful life. If you are reading this book, you understand how important it is to release yourself from the behaviors holding you back from a more fulfilling life.

Growth is part of life. A blade of grass can even grow through cement. Likewise, we can grow despite any circumstance or obstacle we face. Adversity is part of our human journey. It calls us to grow. Growing and adapting when faced with adversity is part of our DNA. Every creature on earth shares that mission—to grow into its purpose. People can choose how they will undertake this task, living life as if it happens to them or living life as if they are conduits. To live in the suffering is to see life only as it is happening to them. They are the recipients of the good and bad without realizing the cause and effect in life's circumstances. They do not see the seed of good in at least the lessons that come from each event. The person who sees life as a gift recognizes that everything life brings is for their growth. They appreciate the unfolding of life.

If a part of you leans toward dwelling in suffering, do not blame or disapprove of yourself; your new realization is to be congratulated. This is the first move to realizing you can make different choices, and the fact is it is part of our nature to see certain situations through the poor me lens; as we become aware of that behavior, we move forward, empowered to live life as it is and experience it with love and acceptance.

A Tale of Two Sisters

Despite being raised by the same parents, in the same home, Juliette and Danette's true stories demonstrate how your reaction to circumstances affects your life and the lives of others.

I am intimately close to these sisters who experienced similar situations in their marriages, which both eventually ended in divorce. Both felt undervalued, unappreciated, and unloved. Each came into her marriage with high self-esteem, a good career, a good-paying job, and good relationships with friends and family. The sisters did not see the resemblance in their husbands to how their father treated them as they grew up; their dad was a chauvinist who undervalued women.

As a side note, we often attract what we are used to and feel comfortable with in our partners. The sisters' experience within their marriages was abusive and destroyed their confidence. When they divorced, they were different women. Juliette divorced after four years of marriage and became a single mom to a one-year-old son. Danette divorced after nine years and had a five-year-old daughter.

Here is where the decisions they made set their lives on very different paths. Juliette chose to dwell in her suffering. She badmouthed her ex-husband and spent her time with those who would listen when she talked about her unfortunate life circumstances. After her divorce, her relationship with her ex-husband dwelled in suffering. She held on to the anger and kept replaying the stories in her head, continuing to be a martyr when talking to her ex-husband about their son. She would give in to the ex-husband's demands about how and when he would see their son. Juliette continued to sustain her suffering, and she allowed her son to see that behavior and make it his own.

Danette chose a different path. Even before her divorce, she sought out help by going to therapy because she did not want to continue the suffering. Counseling was part of the reason she decided to divorce, understanding that maintaining the marriage would lead to more abuse and suffering. After she divorced, she continued counseling for many years because she wanted to know more about herself. She wanted to understand why her marriage failed, how she could be a better mother, and how she could grow from the experience. Her goal was to rise from the experience. Danette's relationship with her ex-husband was amicable, despite initially being resentful. She chose not to speak badly about her ex-husband, especially in front of her daughter. When people asked what happened, she gave a vague answer, saying, "We decided to end it because neither of us was happy anymore." Because of her actions, she and her ex-husband became friends and provided a good example and environment for their daughter. She set her boundaries in their relationship and collected child-support. She understood that setting boundaries is an important part of all relationships, and she showed her daughter this valuable example. She also understood that learning and moving on from the experiences would be better for her and her daughter.

The course each sister took after her divorce affected her child dramatically. Juliette's son grew up watching his parents' animosity toward each other. His father opted to pull back instead of dealing with his ex-wife, so his relationship with his son suffered, which caused the young man to feel his father did not love him. Mother and son commiserated about the relationship. The son's self-image and self-love began to suffer, and by the time he was twelve, his relationship with his father was almost non-existent.

Juliette and her son had a close relationship as he was growing up, but now in his late thirties, they have grown apart. He developed a pattern of running away when he got serious about a love relationships. Although he is a very smart college graduate, he has not chosen to prosper in a career. He carries a lot of unresolved pain and dwells in suffering. His relationship with his mother suffers because they are often at odds, fueling each other's negative beliefs about each other and the world.

Danette's daughter grew up loving and respecting her father. He remarried when she was eight, and she has a good relationship with her stepmother and her siblings from her father's second marriage. Her father always contributed to her wellbeing with child support, has always been part of her life, and contributed to her college tuition. With two loving and involved parents, she graduated from college debt free. The relationship between her parents is friendly and supportive. She has celebrated many milestones with both her parents attending the celebrations. She grew up in an environment that saw difficult events as learning opportunities, not situations that happen to us, so she has adopted the mindset of acceptance. She is an adult who has healthy relationships and looks forward to getting married and having her own family. She has a good relationship with her mother whom she calls her best friend.

Mastering Life

We are meant to grow and flourish, and for some, the way forward is growing their careers by seeking education. In the United States, children from age five to eighteen go to school and learn a preset curriculum. Many continue by attending college or university and learning more about interesting subjects or developing the skills for their chosen careers. This type of learning lends itself to an intellectual way of walking in the world. Intellectually, they are experts in a field of study, and depending on what their chosen occupation is, the time and effort invested in learning generally pays off. Career opportunities open for those who take the time to complete a certain level of education or training. Applying oneself to a field of study is rewarded with a good job, knowledge gained, and the respect of peers for the way one leads their life.

You are the master of your life when it comes to your intellectual self. How do you master other areas?

If you would like to master other areas, decide to grow. Decide to learn from everything around you and view situations and circumstances as learning opportunities presented for the purpose of your growth. As humans, we are perfect beings with tremendous potential to be, to do, to have, and to give what we would love; being open to Life's feedback is a requirement for growth. The school of Life is full of opportunities for growth without having to pick up a book. The opportunities for growth are alive in the experiences you live, in the daily routines, in the person you become, and in the choices you make.

Your journey is filled with learning opportunities. You learn as you go. As a child, you may burn your hand on the stove and learn you must be careful. You learn how to navigate relationships. You learn acceptable behaviors from your parents' feedback. You listen to peers and learn how to communicate and relate to them. You are constantly learning how to navigate life from the feedback you receive from others. And by default, you respond and react to Life as you have seen others do. This is one way you end up thinking life happens to you. By deciding to grow, you will change that perspective and learn that life happens with you, and when you have full awareness, it happens as you. You are life. You are the maker of your own life.

The Law of Motion

The third law of motion according to Isaac Newton states, "To every action there is always opposed an equal reaction." Understanding this law helps us understand the unfolding of the lives of the two sisters described in this chapter. Juliette chose to dwell in the suffering of past events and blamed the situation or other person for what was happening around her. Danette's choice was to learn from her experiences and take responsibility for her actions. The relationship each formed with her respective ex-husband was based on the behavior she chose. Juliette's action to blame and refusal to leave her suffering behind caused a reaction from her ex-husband that severed their relationship and deeply affected her son. On the other hand, Danette's actions to learn from the experience and move forward contributed to her ex-husband's reaction to continue a relationship and was a positive experience for her daughter.

The way these sisters' lives played out demonstrates how our actions play out. The way each sister dealt with her situation set the tone for the relationship she and her respective child had with the other parent. Mahatma Gandhi said, "You must be the change you want to see in the world." This statement resonates with people who understand their actions create the reality they seek.

When you want to change something, you must start with you. If you would like to change the way a person is in a relationship, your actions can cause that change. You only have control over your own actions, but your actions set off the other person's reactions. Change the part of yourself that is focusing on what you don't want because life reflects what you put forth. You hold the key to how other people treat you and respond to you, and in a broader way, you hold the key to how events and situations transpire. When you hold on to suffering, you continue to relive and blame, but when you let go and become accountable for your life, the flow of life changes. You shift your paradigm from constrictive to expansive and begin to experience your world differently.

Resisting Change

"The only constant in life is change" is a clever way of acknowledging the constant evolution of all things. If you are not changing, then you are not growing. It takes courage to change, and it is rigorous work requiring being aware of the aspects of yourself you are shedding and what you are adopting. It requires being diligent and determined to do the work of shifting the thoughts, feelings, and habits that no longer feel like you to ones you would love to have or be.

Most importantly, it requires acknowledging you are not perfect—you are a work in progress in a process that requires self-acceptance and release of the ego.

Once you accept yourself, you open yourself to the possibility of changing, of creating new thoughts, behaviors, and emotions. Adopting this perspective allows you to co-create with Infinite Intelligence and flow with Life. You move into the flow of Life innate to other living things—the natural immersion of growing into a new version of their becoming. As part of the human species, you have a choice to decide to grow; deciding to grow is the beginning of evolving into your purpose. And when you refuse growth, Life has a natural way of helping that, in some cases, can turn into suffering.

If you are not ready for change, or open to embracing and accepting growth, a situation or condition may push you toward what you are resisting. Because we are creatures of evolution, life's circumstances work to push us in the direction of growth. Unless you change, life will continue to provide experiences that nudge you to move in a different direction. Learning to listen to life's whispers and nudges is part of growth. Learning to listen to the discontent in your life and observe what you are longing for is part of the formula that leads to growth. What tends to happen when you don't listen to life's signals is life gets more difficult. You do not enjoy that part of life; relationships start falling apart, difficult people come into your life, and illnesses may be revealed. You feel like you keep bumping against a brick wall no matter what you do. Those are the times when you are called to surrender to life.

Surrendering to Life

For the last ten years of my corporate work, I heard a voice in my head saying, "Is this all there is to life?" It was questioning my existence and contribution to life. I was enjoying my job, the people, the income, the commute, and the freedom it brought me, yet something was missing. I felt I was not leaving a legacy to humanity. The question asked by the part of me that wanted more lived within for years until life became difficult. I was promoted, and my new boss' actions led me to work harder, longer hours, become less confident, and eventually suffer anxiety. I would have anxiety attacks while enjoying time with family, and I suffered from insomnia. Life was pushing me to listen to the voice and discover a new version of me. I had not paid attention to the voice initially, so situations in my life manifested to make me uncomfortable enough to entertain change.

I set out with the intention of finding the answer by enriching my spiritual life with meditation and studying *A Course in Miracles* and other books. As I aligned with my inner self, I asked Spirit to guide me to find the answer. Even though I understood there was something more for me, I still refused to leave my job; I was taking steps spiritually but not in my career, which is where growth was asking to be birthed. And then I was amazed when Life spoke by ending my employment. It was a great transition to help me discover what was yearning to grow within me. I knew I wanted to be of service to others, but I did not know what that looked like.

I used my intellect to move to a non-profit organization, thinking that would fill the void in my soul. Surprisingly, I discovered it did not. Yes, I was happy serving the homeless, immigrants, and later the employees of the organization, but still, the voice would not retire. I could not let go of the thought, the feeling, the intuition that there was something I was required to do. Rumi's words resonated with me: "It's as if a king has sent you to some country to do a task, and you perform a hundred other services, but not the one he sent you to do." That set me on track to finding what I am called to do.

The discovery process was interesting because I expected to hear from my inner self in meditation or somehow to be inspired. I have no doubt Spirit was making my goal known, yet I was not hearing the answer as I continued with the business of my current job.

One morning, I woke up impatient to know and loudly yelled to the sky, "Please let me know today—what is my next step? What am I here to do?"

That day, I was consciously paying attention to everything around me—road signs, conversations with people, material on social media—because I knew I would get an answer. While driving, the podcast I was listening to finished, and without paying much attention to the choices, I turned on a podcast where a woman was asking five questions about "Are you a person who…?" Each question described a quality or characteristic that described me. Then she said, "Then you should consider life coaching as a career."

I had never heard of life coaching and did not know what it was. I looked up at the sky as if Spirit were up there and said, "Are you talking to me? Is this what I am supposed to do?" That day, I went home and researched life coaching; in my gut, I knew it was for me. I knew I had finally heard the answer.

The next step was to look for a school since I had learned there are many approaches to life coaching. Which approach did Spirit have in mind for me? I did an internet search and was bombarded with messages, videos, and a slew of overwhelming information. Again, I asked for Spirit's guidance in finding the school that would be best for me, and behold, I received an email that led to the Life Mastery Institute, now called Brave Thinking Institute, and Mary Morrisey.

I scheduled a call for a Saturday morning. I was sitting in my atrium waiting for the call when a dragonfly flew in. I have a relationship with nature and take "coincidences or chances" in nature as messages from Spirit. Over the years, through my Native American study of totem animal beliefs, I've developed the ability to interpret the messages. I interpreted the dragonfly as a sign of transformation and self-realization. When I started my conversation, the dragonfly flew out. After about an hour, the representative asked me to join their course. I hesitated because it was a big investment, more than I was comfortable with without talking to my husband. I am in a supportive marriage now, and we have set agreements on our expenditures. As I was pressed for a decision, I saw the dragonfly flying directly toward me and reentering the atrium. That was a sign from Infinite Intelligence that I should do this, and I did.

The wonderful thing about making a decision supported by God is that everything will align. When I spoke with my husband Daniel, he was fully supportive. Despite the amount, I had no buyer's remorse. I was calm and confident on the path. Because of how I felt, I knew I had landed on the right course. It was a rare experience at the time to feel so connected and aligned with Spirit. Up until that moment, I had experienced moments of alignment, and since then I have grown to live in that space more often. This feeling was like the time I spent walking with my health (cancer) journey. I knew it was exactly what I was supposed to be experiencing at that time. When you are aligned with purpose, you have a peace and grace that allows you to walk with love—it is almost as if you are watching yourself go through the process.

I share this story so you can appreciate how decision making is supported by Spirit when you are acting for your highest good. When you open yourself to growing, fear will play a role in your decisions. The paradigms that keep you from moving forward rise up since you are moving into unfamiliar territory; you are welcoming becoming someone new. These feelings are normal in the human journey. As you saw in my story, I depended on my gut, my intuition, and the signs to help me jump from where I was to where I wanted to be.

In the beginning of my journey, I was forced into change because I was not listening to my longing. Life was speaking loud and clear with the emergence of physical symptoms due to the toxic relationship with my boss, but I was refusing to listen because I was comfortable with other aspects of my job. In fact, I was enjoying my work despite the anxiety. The financial aspect also kept me tied to that job. The security of a paycheck brought comfortable living.

Trusting and expecting things will work out is part of the formula. You know you are supported by the Universe when you are walking in fulfillment of your purpose and dream. As you begin to navigate your journey, you will find Life speaks to you directly and personally, giving you signals only you will understand. Fear will continue to peek into the process, yet the more you believe, trust, and expect, the more comfort you will feel as you walk with life.

Exercise

This exercise is to help you change an aspect of yourself you know is not serving you.

1. Identify a person who has the quality(ies) you would love to adopt. You see this person having the relationships you would love and know it is because they have a certain quality you don't currently have.

    For example: Your work relationships are not as friendly and nurturing as you would like, and you see that a coworker has the types of relationships you would love to have. Observe your coworker to identify the behaviors working for them that you may be missing. For instance, is the person a better listener, less judgmental, or more giving of time or compliments? What is it about them that others enjoy and are attracted to so they have a better relationship?

As you observe, do it with curiosity and admiration, not with envy or judgment.

Identify the person and their qualities:

_____

_____

_____

_____

2. Identify the differences in your behavior compared to that person. Play a movie in your head, observing how you act and how they act. What behaviors do you need to change? This should be done without judgment. Congratulate yourself on your awareness and desire to feel better about who you are.

_____

_____

_____

_____

_____

3. Once you've recognized the differences—what you would love to change (behavior A), and what you would love to adopt (behavior B)—pinpoint when in your daily routine you exhibit the behavior that no longer serves you.

4. Start replacing behavior A with behavior B when performing the routines or in the situations you've identified.

As you start making these changes, you will discover other instances and other behaviors you would substitute. This is a process. Be patient, kind, and willing to continue to experiment and you will be surprised by the results.

Summary

Abraham Maslow said it best: "In any given moment we have two options: to step forward into growth or step back into safety." Staying in your safety zone will initially feel comfortable, yet eventually lead to stress since the natural way of life is to grow. Deciding to grow is rigorous work because it requires a commitment to constant change and development. In the journey you undertake, you will face many fears. The thing to do is to befriend your fears by facing them. The more you face them, the more comfortable you will become in your process.

You will encounter failure as well, so changing your perspective on how you see failure will empower you to continue. When Thomas Edison was asked how it felt to have failed 10,000 times while inventing the incandescent light bulb, he said, "I have not failed. I've just found 10,000 ways that won't work." Life is a trial-and-error process. Especially when we are in the middle of it, we may miss the obvious, but that is all right. We keep trying.

The key to facing failure is to acknowledge it and move forward in the process as quickly as possible. Giving it energy only makes it tougher to get out of the contractive energy. The key to success is accepting fear and failure along the way—both are here to teach us and empower us (in an odd way) to succeed. I see them as guardrails—something to avoid, yet useful in better understanding our process, our progress, and ourselves.

The main and most important thing is to make the decision and start taking small steps. Small steps, one by one, lead to tremendous growth. Once you start moving forward, you will see changes in yourself you would never have imagined. You will develop a sense of trust in the perfection of life. Everything that happens is for your highest good. The Universe is aligning opportunity for you, assisting you with coincidences, synchronicities, and signs to reassure you that you are on the right course. You will begin to trust your decisions and live a more fulfilling life in flow with the Universe.

"We have within us, a power that is greater than anything we shall ever contact in the outer, a power that can overcome every obstacle in our life and set us safe, satisfied, and at peace, healed and prosperous, in a new light, and in a new life."

— Ernest Holmes

Chapter 4

Being Curious

"I have no special talents. I am only

passionately curious."

— Albert Einstein

While growing into your purpose, passion, and happiness sounds exciting, deciding to do so is also scary since it may lead to surprises, unexpected outcomes, or in some cases, a blind leap of faith that you will end up where you are supposed to be. Or you may have the monkey mind asking a thousand and one questions about your decision and second guessing it along the way. How will you know you are going in the right direction? How will you know the decisions you are making are leading to the right place? Your analytical brain asks questions to protect and deter you from moving forward with ideas or decisions that may feel baseless or just different. Your analytical mind focusses on what you experience from the five senses; if it does not see evidence of victory on the horizon, it wants to keep you in a familiar zone so it will cast fear and doubt on your next steps. The paradigms you have developed work to keep you stagnant and, in your routines, dissuading you from discovering your true self and growing.

As children, most of us had no experience of failure, loss, or hurt, and our analytical brain didn't hinder our exploration of new things in a desire to protect us. We had a quality that helped us grow and stay motivated to seek more experiences—that quality was curiosity. Curiosity was the key that opened the door to a new world that introduced us to new experiences and new information. It led to discovering our likes and dislikes. It led us down a path of wonder, joy, and surprises.

Around the same time, while curiosity was alive as the gate to discovery and learning, our imagination saw vast opportunities, and everything was possible. Imagination allowed us to dream without limit and trust our dreams were possible. We found joy in this state of full trust, fantasy, creativity, and discovery. It had a pureness of living a reality with no obstacles and constraints on what was possible.

Your young self's natural curiosity prompted you to listen to conversations between people and ask questions. You paid attention to your surroundings and wondered why things were the way they were. You experimented by taking things apart without caring if you could put them back together. You were not deterred, and you loved discovering new information that fed your mind and left you wanting more. You were, in fact, connected to your inner wisdom and followed it. You were not afraid of where the discovery would lead because you had an undeveloped analytical mind. Your actions were not guided by your five senses but by the pure desire to learn and grow. You had a child's innocence that made you trust without fear—no problems, just total trust in everything and everyone around you. You had a wholesome trust in Infinite. (Although at that age you may not have been aware of Infinite Intelligence, an innate trust existed within you.)

Then what happened? As you grew, your curiosity may have waned, possibly because of the feedback and discouragement you received from adults. As a child, in your path of discovery, you likely asked questions adults had difficulty answering. The old saying "Curiosity killed the cat" is a warning against being too curious.

In the same way as curiosity was repressed, imagination was constrained because your analytical mind took center stage. You had experiences with failure, hurt, fear, and established paradigms for your safety. Your curiosity may have faded, your innocence vanished, and you became less connected with your inner wisdom and Infinite

Source. You became more dependent on your five senses and your analytical mind to direct your journey.

Walt Whitman said, "Be curious, not judgmental." Curiosity is the place you must open yourself up to and live from if you are seeking growth. As an adult, this may be a switch in your brain that needs to be turned on to awaken the part of yourself leading to self-awareness. It may be a habit that needs to be nurtured by asking questions every step of the way. It is easy to be inquisitive when good things are happening, but it is rigorous work when you are undergoing challenges. The seemingly easy way to deal with a challenge is to feel sad and regretful, while sharing your misfortune with others. If you are on a healing and growing journey, you must overcome such behaviors. Setting the intention to stay awake to lessons being put in front of you by way of a challenge, you open yourself up to being and staying curious, which will allow you to discover things about yourself that will lead to healing and growing.

Being curious must be done in a way compatible with how you were as a child—open to the wonder and fascination of discovery. A feeling of expansion comes with the energy that brings the answer directly from Infinite Intelligence God Source. That expansion realigns you with your inner wisdom and knowing the answer from the inside out.

Being curious is like a direct connection with Spirit that leads you to your truth, the truth you need to hear as a golden nugget from the experience you are facing. That truth will lead you to more understanding and thereby make your experience more valuable and spiritual. You will understand there is a connection between your past and your current circumstance, making it easier to live more intentionally focused on what you want to create in the future. You see the challenge as the fruit of the past, and you learn that what you do today is the only thing you can control, the only thing that matters. It also encourages you to change your mindset since you realize the consequence of default living. Default living is living without intention about what will be, without a dream of what can be, only reacting to what is happening now.

Now that you understand the connection of your past to your now, you can live from your now for the dream future you would love. Today is when you build the rest of your life, stop being a victim of circumstance, and accept with no judgment the challenges before you.

Jane's Lightbulb Moment

In a previous chapter, you read about Jane and the health challenges she faces. She is a student of the *spiritual laws* and is committed to becoming healthier and having a more joyful life enjoying vibrant, dynamic health. In her quest to manifest a healthier body, Jane became curious about what prompted her many illnesses. It was not genetics since most of her family enjoys good health. She told me in her open curiosity and openness to the answer, she had a lightbulb moment—a moment when the answer to what you are wondering about comes to you with clarity and understanding. It's knowledge you already had, but somehow, it is covered in the shadows of your subconscious.

Jane's lightbulb moment revealed that her illnesses were linked to her childhood. She had been part of a troubled family, so getting her mother's attention had been difficult. Jane, at a young age, discovered when she was ill, her mom gave her undivided attention. Her mother would nurture and care for her and provide the love she craved. When she was in school, she remembers faking illnesses to stay home and receive her mother's love and care. Jane missed a lot of school that way. This pattern continued into her adult life.

What an amazing discovery for Jane. Finding her truth about why she had been battling poor health her whole life opened the door to recovery. She can start healing as she works on breaking down the paradigms preventing good health. She understands her illnesses are deeply rooted in her need to be loved. Now she can find resources to help her override her subconscious need to be sick.

Curiosity Is the Gateway to Understanding

When you become curious, you learn, you discover, you grow, and you are free to move forward. Jane's story illustrates how becoming curious opened the channel of awareness into her life and the paradigms she mastered. By knowing that what she had been thinking and doing as a child was connected to her experiences of today, she can concentrate on healing the wounds of her childhood and change her behaviors, which will lead to improving her health.

The point of becoming curious is to see your life as a vehicle for learning and becoming a better you, to see life as an opportunity to master the self, to get to know yourself better, and to unite with your higher self. When you become curious about why you are navigating a certain path, you will be given the answers that allow growth. Trust that curiosity will lead you toward your higher self, just like when you were a small child and you trusted that being curious would lead to more understanding about the world around you.

Before you can use curiosity as the gateway to understanding and growth, you need to accept the power of Infinite Intelligence and surrender control for at least a moment. For a moment, know there is a Higher Being able to provide all answers, and being curious opens your energy to receiving the information you seek. For example, as you navigate a challenging situation, the immediate questions are: Why me? How can this happen? Those questions keep you stuck in the energy of the condition you are facing. But if you ask a "what" question, you open the energy to receiving guidance. Your question can be, "What is seeking to emerge from this condition? What is this all about? What can I learn from this situation? What can I do to remain open to discovery? What golden nuggets are laid out for me to pick up and learn from? What is Life telling me? You will be given the answer via light-bulb moments, Spirit talking through other people or your surroundings, or you will simply know the answer from your intuition and higher self.

Curiosity leads to comprehending why you are navigating the terrain, recognizing the lesson as it is given, and understanding there is Infinite Intelligence in all that happens. All things happen for a reason. From the human perspective, you may not know the answer, but you can learn it by staying curious.

My Own Lightbulb Moment

As I write this book, I am undergoing breast cancer treatment. I have had sixteen rounds of chemotherapy, and I am recuperating from a partial mastectomy and reconstruction surgery. The motivation for this book was sharing my story as a breast cancer patient using the principles I've learned and that I teach and practice as a life coach. During this journey, I have met many women who endured much pain, physically and emotionally, while being treated for cancer. I have seen how the principles I practice as a life coach have helped me navigate my journey with less stress and pain. Many of the medical practitioners I've had the privilege of working with have also seen and commented on the difference between me and other patients. This has inspired me to share the principles, my journey, and the tools so others traversing an illness can benefit.

One Friday evening in July of 2020, after my husband Daniel and I finished dinner, we were admiring nature in our atrium when the doctor called. I'd had a biopsy earlier in the week and was expecting to see negative results on my online chart. Despite my optimism about the biopsy, it was bad news. My doctor apologized for the diagnosis and was truly empathetic about what was ahead in my journey. He asked me not to worry and provided referrals for oncology treatment.

As I now play the conversation back in my head, I am still surprised by my response. I was so calm. I even told the doctor everything was fine, that I knew I was going to be okay, and I thanked him for his generous empathy and care. Something inside kept me calm. My heart, my spirit, everything within me knew this was a season of learning for me. I had no idea what the future would hold, but I knew God was working for my good. I felt protected, at ease. I knew there was a reason I was being presented with the journey ahead.

I realized my reaction was uncommon. Until then, I'd had no health issues, no health-crushing, life-changing diagnosis. I am still surprised at my reaction, since I skipped the first four steps of grief altogether—no denial, anger, bargaining, or depression—and went straight to acceptance. Although fear, doubt, and despair were part of my experience, I did not allow them to take over. I was instead full of curiosity and interest about what the future would hold and how my life would evolve and change. I was fascinated by what would evolve and what Spirit's purposeful lesson would be for me. Like Jane, I was also curious about the disease's origin; how had it come to be in my body when I had always been healthy and had no genetic predisposition to cancer? I quickly opened myself to hearing the answer, to understanding how I had manifested cancer.

I knew there was a reason breast cancer was part of my life, so I asked Spirit for the answer, knowing it would come. Within a few days, as I was getting dressed one morning, I heard myself thinking, *I wish I had smaller breasts* as I was putting on my bra. I stopped and did a double-take on my own thoughts, knowing it was the answer. For almost thirty years, I had said that in my mind thousands of times—getting dressed, trying on clothes, seeing myself in pictures, or passing by a store window. I even said it to myself when part of my lunch would land on my well-endowed torso. And every morning, as I put on my bra, that was my thought. "No wonder!" I said out loud and then told Daniel what I had discovered.

As a life coach, I know your thoughts lead to your feelings, which lead to your emotions, leading to your actions, which lead to your results. The reason I manifested breast cancer was because, for the last thirty years, I had been telling myself I was dissatisfied with my own body, specifically my breasts.

I was dealing with a paradigm that had come alive when I was a teller at a credit union. I sat on a tall stool with just the upper portion of my body visible. I was a young, petite woman with large breasts, and when some men came to the window, I would catch them looking at my breasts. I did not like that kind of attention. I became very conscious of it and started to dislike my chest area. My dissatisfaction with my body was reinforced when buying clothes. I had to buy larger dresses and have them tailored, eventually switching to pants and shirts since I could buy smaller pants and larger shirts. This paradigm also caused me to gain weight to hide a figure that attracted male attention. To give you a visual on my physique, my bra size was DDD/F, which is an extra-large, and my pants were size six, which is small. As you may imagine, I wanted to change my appearance; therefore, I reinforced the desire for smaller breasts daily while dressing.

Being curious and open to learning the reason for my breast cancer led me to me becoming more aware of my daily thoughts. I made sure that wish for smaller breasts was not repeated. Instead of the voice in my head wishing for a different figure, I daily tell my body I love it. This may not cure the disease, but it is helping me heal. It reminds me I must be aware of my thoughts because they will manifest my tomorrow. This realization without judgment allowed me to take responsibility for the disease and continue to gather golden nuggets that will help me become a better person and better coach. I am, as I traverse new experiences of treatment, learning daily how best to navigate this experience so others can benefit from the practices I share in this book.

This story is a difficult one to share because I do not want you to blame yourself for the illnesses you've encountered or are experiencing. My objective is to demonstrate how staying open and curious to the answers you want will lead you to those answers. Curiosity adds to your understanding and growth. Staying inquisitive about your journey often leads to clarity, enlightenment, and understanding.

Enjoying the Path of Curiosity

Walt Disney said, "We keep moving forward, opening new doors, and doing new things, because we are curious, and curiosity keeps leading us down new paths."

By remaining curious, you keep moving and growing; one answer leads to another question and then yet another answer. It makes life interesting and fun. It is a way to flow with life and learn from the experiences you are living. By choosing to be curious, you are open to the adventure in all experiences. All experiences are manifested by and are teaching from Infinite God Source, and the best way to encounter them is by staying curious.

Curiosity is the vehicle to understanding; when you stay curious, you stay open to learning. It's as if you open the flow of information (without regard to the outcome) and receive the answers. Take the example of Jane discovering the source of her illnesses was in her childhood beliefs, and my story of connecting my thoughts about having large breasts and manifesting breast cancer. These two examples reveal how wondering about things can lead to unfolding the layers that make up who you are and the circumstances and situations you face.

It also leads to making better choices in what to think, feel, and believe, and to challenging yourself to stay awake today to the thoughts you want to be your results tomorrow. It is like knowing every thought and feeling is a seedling for the opportunities in front of you.

Discover Your Purpose

Some people are born knowing exactly what they are meant to do in this lifetime. Others, like me, have tried and done many things and continued to wonder what our purpose is. I have had many jobs, yet despite enjoying them, I still wondered how I could fulfill my higher purpose. After years of feeling there had to be more to life than what I was doing, I finally allowed myself to surrender to the question. I intentionally committed to finding what would fulfill my purpose and assure my inner wisdom that I was here for a special reason. I was always curious, yet once I was determined to know the answer, I was led to life coaching. It took time, exploration, and willingness to do what needed to be done as I felt the nudges and heard the call, but it mostly took being and staying curious with "an open hand" on what could be. What I mean by "an open hand" is my willingness to let go of the expectations and remain open to finding the answer.

The initial call was to leave my corporate job, and clearly, I did not see the disembark sign quickly, but after being laid off, I knew despite the pay involved in my previous career, I could not go back to a corporate environment, so I chose a non-profit. What I heard from my intuition was that my calling was to serve people. I did it. I tried it, and still I was unfulfilled, but my inner wisdom continued to say, "Serve others," so if I was not serving them in a non-profit, what did that mean? I had no idea, so I continued to be curious and stay open to the possibilities, which led to a career I didn't even know existed.

Rumi said, "Let the beauty of what you love be what you do." I think this is your biggest clue when finding your purpose—do what you love. Stay curious because what you love will change or evolve and staying curious will lead to growth, joy, and purpose. When you are curious, you continue to receive the energy to acquire information from Infinite God Source. It is like talking with a friend—if you stay open, intrigued, and curious, you enjoy the conversation and learn from your friend. If you are multi-tasking and not really involved and engaged, you will miss some of the best parts of the conversation. That is how being and staying curious works. It is like leaving the door wide open for whatever you are to experience.

Some of my clients when I first met them did not know what they would love. They had shut down the part of themselves that is allowed to dream and discover. I noticed that in their familial relationships, they were seen as the responsible one or the person others depended on. They had followed the path that was reasonable, lucrative, and best for their family's welfare. They hadn't been in touch with their longing or discontent or allowed themselves to be curious about what was emerging inside of them. Where was Spirit leading them? What did their heart desire? What would they love?

Allowing themselves to dream was challenging not only because it was something new for them, but it also felt vulnerable to listen to a part of themselves that had not been previously recognized. In these cases, the discovery birthed amazing visions of a life that otherwise never would have appeared.

Remember when you were a little kid and trusted your curiosity, indifferent to consequences because you were unaware of what could go wrong. That energy and perception will help you maintain the curiosity that will lead you to growth and purpose.

Exercise A

Notice your thoughts and actions when you are looking for the answer to why an unwanted situation has appeared in your life.

When the situation arises, do the following:

1. Acknowledge there is a Higher Being, Infinite Intelligence, that

knows and understands the reason for the condition. This can be a single thought of acknowledgment and understanding or a daily prayer that leads you to that understanding.

2. Know that everything around you is happening because of this Intelligent Being.

3. Become curious about what could have brought the situation into being and/or what you are to learn from it.

4. Find a quiet space and a quiet place within yourself where you will feel you are being heard.

5. Ask, I wonder what _____ [fill in the blank]?

6. Set the intention of knowing the answer by a certain day, within the week, etc.

7. Stay open to hearing the answer as you go about your day(s).

   a. Notice what you begin noticing about your daily thoughts, feelings, and actions. The answer may be in your awareness of how you are flowing with life.

   b. Notice what you begin noticing around you—signs, people, conversations, nature, social media. You may see a sign, hear someone say something, receive an idea/thought. Write it down if need be to analyze it and take it in.

c. The answer is within you; your request to know the answer
and remain open to it brings it forth.

Exercise B

Perform all the steps up to number six above and journal the answers, writing everything that comes to mind. Use a separate piece
of paper since it may take several pages. Give yourself at least twenty minutes of uninterrupted journaling time. Keep writing even
when nothing comes to mind. Just write anything and everything
you think. The answer will come as you remain patient and open. Do
not analyze or evaluate what you are writing. Using your analytical
mind when doing this exercise will disrupt the outcome.

Once you have finished writing, read it and highlight what resonates
with you. Which parts of the text jump off the page or feel true when
you read them?

Summary

Steve Jobs said, "Much of what I stumbled into by following my curiosity and intuition turned out to be priceless later on."

We need curiosity the most during times of adversity. I have found as I navigate breast cancer that when I am feeling low or uncomfortable, or a side effect from the treatment manifests, I can use curiosity to stop that feeling. This is when questioning becomes even more valuable and noticing what you are noticing about your thoughts, feelings, and actions is most important because it cuts the flow of energy to the symptom and focuses it on doing something about it. When the cancer or its treatments have you down, imagine how it feels to be in great health and ask, "What can I do to feel better?" You will hear a whisper pointing you to at least one thing that can turn the situation from bad to good or tolerable. I have had few symptoms associated with the treatments because I continue to be curious. When I felt nausea and asked the question, I thought of breathing, and after breathing, another answer would come and allow me to counter the symptom. When I felt lethargic and asked the question, the answer was counterintuitive, but I was still able to counter the symptom by going for a walk around the block—fresh air, oxygen, and the beauty of nature brought me to feeling gratitude. When I displayed moodiness, I asked the question, and again the answer was to admire nature in some way since the beauty of nature releases endorphins, giving me a happiness boost.

If you have lost your curiosity gene, it is time to regenerate it and cultivate it. I love what Albert Einstein has to say about being curious: "I have not special talents, I'm only passionately curious." I believe curiosity opens us up to hear from our intuitive genius.

Chapter 5

Examining Your Perception

"We see the world not as it is, but as we are. When we describe what we see, we in effect describe ourselves. When people disagree with us, we think something is wrong with them. Changing our perception takes great effort."

— Stephen Covey, *The 7 Habits of Highly Effective People*

While being curious about what is happening in your life draws fresh ideas, thoughts, and conclusions, it also brings a new perspective. The framework of that perspective is tied to your own perception of the world. Perception is defined as the ability to see, hear, or become aware of something through the senses, and it is a way of regarding, understanding, or interpreting something. It is the mental impression you formulate about the world around you. Learning to examine your perception and being open to shifting it allows you to expand and bring more dimension to your reality. Perception is a limited faculty that when shifted can lead to limitless possibilities. The way you use perception, as a mental faculty, is key in changing your reality and, in turn, changing the way you interact with the world.

Your perception was born from your paradigms, which are the multitude of ideas embedded in your subconscious from what you were taught as a child and your experiences. Those paradigms cause you to look at the world in a certain way, which has given birth to your reality. If you have a tendency to look at yourself as non-deserving, you have a paradigm focused on unworthiness. Your perspective on yourself affects your entire existence, as does the perceptions you have of others and the world around you.

Shifting your perception is not an easy task because, as we move through life, we experience different emotions and beliefs that create our perceptions. Imagine yourself walking down a busy street full of people coming and going in different directions. You can see their facial expressions and can only guess what is going on in their lives. Each person is deep in thought about what they just experienced. A young person is smiling because they are thinking about the interview they just had for their dream job, and they know they did well. An elderly person is crossing the street looking grouchy because each step causes physical pain and their spouse of sixty-five years is in the hospital. A middle-aged person has a seriously worried look and is deep in thought as they wonder how, as a single parent of three, they will make ends meet. A young couple is almost skipping down the street, holding hands because they decided to play hooky from school and spend the day in the park. Each person has an expression on their face as they walk past you on the street and make eye contact. You can interpret their expression as a welcoming, happy greeting or a nasty look as if you did something to offend them. Each person is actually in their own reality and their expression has nothing to do with you. Your perception makes it about you.

I became aware of this fact when I read *The Four Agreements*. One agreement is "Don't take anything personally." It reminds us nothing others do is because of us. Since then, it has been easier to understand people's actions and reactions have nothing to do with us, so why take anything personally and make it about us? Changing our perception and embracing this fact liberates us from suffering. This is an easy concept to understand until we have a relationship that is not doing well or a disagreement with someone we care about. Then, it becomes more difficult to avoid making it about us.

The Store Clerk

Mary Morrissey tells a story that illustrates how our perception plays a role in how we feel about and see things. Mary describes a trip to the grocery store. When she was in the checkout line, she saw that the clerk appeared to be upset. When it was Mary's turn, she noticed the clerk scanned some items twice and pointed it out. The clerk grabbed the receipt from Mary's hand and, huffing and puffing, addressed the error. Mary noticed the clerk was not very friendly or enjoying her work. Mary's perception was perhaps this person should not be a grocery store clerk. Once Mary completed the transaction, a young bagger helped her get her groceries to her car. She offhandedly mentioned the clerk appeared to be having a terrible day. The bagger said, "Oh, yes! It is terrible. She shouldn't even be working right now. Her son is in the hospital. He was in a car accident yesterday. She is going through so much right now." Mary's perspective of the clerk changed immediately. She realized the woman was navigating an exceedingly difficult situation. Mary understood why the woman's behavior had nothing to do with liking or not liking her job. It was all about what she was feeling about working while her son was in the hospital. Mary's feelings about the clerk quickly changed from judgment to compassion and empathy.

When you change your perception, you change your reality. One of the late motivational speaker Wayne Dyer's most famous quotes is, "Change the way you look at things, and the things you look at change." The way you feel, think, and see the world changes once you understand your point of view is just that—a point of view. It is not the truth but one point among many points of view. Remaining open to seeing, feeling, and thinking differently expands your world, opening you to the abundance it has to offer. It is like changing your vision from the granular to the universal, from the microscopic to the bird's eye view where you can see much more than what you saw before. Having the capacity to change your perception and remain open to interacting with Life differently can change or even save your life. The story below demonstrates how a change in perception can be lifesaving.

Grief Turned Into Illness

As a child, Joseph was very attached to his mother. When his mom had a daycare, Joseph would be right there following his mom every around every day as she cared for the other kids. When Joseph was in high school, his mother was diagnosed with lung cancer. At first, her prognosis was good, which, of course, was of great relief to the entire family. But they soon discovered his mother could not tolerate the chemotherapy. All they could do was enjoy their time with her until the cancer took her away when Joseph was seventeen. As you can imagine, Joseph's grief was unbearable, and the entire family was devasted.

Joseph's father tried to cope and help his children deal with their grief as he dealt with his own. He tried to get them all counseling, which they tried, but not as a long-term treatment. Each family member settled into their way of dealing with the loss. Joseph chose to mourn quietly and internalize the pain. As an adult, he filled the void his mother left with retail therapy. He had an insatiable hunger for things, for clothes, for anything material. He also had difficulty with commitment. He enjoyed romantic relationships, but when they became serious, he ended the relationships.

When Joseph was in his mid-twenties, he became ill. At first, his illness was a mystery, but eventually, he was diagnosed and treated for a blood disorder that caused his T-cell count to drop, compromising his immune system. Joseph was wary of Western medicine. He could not trust his doctors and refused to take the medicines they prescribed. His father was very worried and asked if he and his stepmom could go to an upcoming doctor's appointment. Joseph agreed since his condition was becoming chronic, as attested to by his weight loss and other symptoms. While the T-cell count of a healthy person is between 500 and 1,600, Joseph's had dropped into the double digits.

Joseph, his dad, and stepmom went to the appointment together. The doctor explained how imperative it was for Joseph to take the prescribed treatment. Joseph's stepmother asked if there was any way of knowing how long his cells had been declining. The doctor turned to the computer and looked in the archives for Joseph's history. He was pleasantly surprised to find a yearly record of Joseph's blood count. The doctor turned the monitor toward Joseph, his father, and stepmom, showing them how each year since October 2006, the T-cell count had been dropping, in essence for the last ten years. They left the doctor's office knowing that an unknown cause was undermining Joseph's blood cells.

When Joseph came to see me, I asked him if he remembered what was going on back when the condition started. It was, of course, when his mom had passed away. Since I have been studying universal principles for many years, I knew his illness was associated with his grief. I equipped Joseph with reading material, meditations, and a perspective that allowed him to change his thought patterns and beliefs and to realize his grief was affecting his health.

Joseph changed his thoughts, and although losing his mom is still a deep wound, he looks at it differently now and has been able to transform his life. Retail therapy is no longer a go-to instinct to numb his hurt. He also understands that pushing people away to avoid commitment will not lead to a happy life. He is now healthy and in a committed relationship.

It is important to understand that Joseph's transformation was not instant. But how he viewed his loss changed, which started his transformation in other areas, including his health.

William Shakespeare said, "Nothing is either good or bad, but thinking makes it so." Shakespeare's idea is clear—how you perceive a situation directly affects how you experience life. If you perceive a situation as good or bad, that is exactly how it will be. Even the toughest of situations can be made better when you shift your perception. While navigating the breast cancer treatments, I was able to discover the truth of this statement.

Shifting Perception of a Deadly Disease

How can anyone see a deadly disease as a good thing? How can contending with fear, anxiety, and physical effects be good? But seeing it as a good thing was the only way I could see it. The alternative would lead to suffering and martyrdom, so to maintain the good in life, choosing to see cancer as a health journey was the most important thing I did.

It all began with changing the name of the journey from "I am a breast cancer patient" to "I am navigating a health journey." When you change the way you look at a thing, the thing itself changes.

Calling it a health journey gave me a sense of power to restore my health and diffused the why me aspect of being a cancer patient. This was such a simple, yet powerful step, and it allowed me to have a more positive experience. By calling it a health journey, my curiosity about what I could do to have better health was piqued, and it led me to ideas about nutrition, exercise, and other means of taking care of my body while I was being treated. That one change in perception was a one-degree move that over time changed the trajectory of my experience to one leading to fewer side effects, and when the chemotherapy ended, my blood test results showed I was healthier than when I had started.

Exercise A

1. Think of a situation or condition you currently perceive as bad or an experience when you took something personally.

2. Write down the issue you recalled.

3. Decide to shift your perspective.

4. Write down all the things that could possibly be good about the situation or a different point of view on the situation you took personally—did the person really mean it to be about you? What other possibilities are there?

5. Examine what you wrote, and in your mind, advocate for the position that it was a good thing.

6. As you advocate for that position, you see yourself believing and shifting your perception about the situation.

7. Disregard ego if ego is getting in the way of shifting your perception. This may be a rigorous process, but the more you do it, the easier it is.

8. As you do this exercise more often, it will become your go-to perspective and allow you to be open to the possibility of finding what good can come from a given situation and choose to hold this new perspective. When you have interactions with others, you will know not everything is about you.

_____

_____

_____

_____

_____

_____

_____

_____

Exercise B

1. Examine your perspective to see if you have chosen a why me perspective in any areas.

2. Write the script you are telling yourself. For example, "My boss has it in for me," or "I am overworked and underpaid," or "I always choose the wrong person."

3. Look at the statement to see how you can change the script by shifting your perspective.

    Shift the perspective scripts:

    a. "My boss has it in for me" to "I am doing an excellent job, and my work is appreciated."

    b. "I am overworked and underpaid" to "I am doing my best work and receive excellent compensation."

    c. "I always choose the wrong person" to "My relationship choices are here to teach me more about me and lead me to finding the love of my life. I make good choices."

4. The new perspective scripts may not appear to be genuine at first, but by shifting your viewpoint, you are in fact attracting a different set of circumstances.

Summary

Albert Einstein said, "There are two ways to live life. One is as though nothing is a miracle. The other is as though everything is a miracle." This is how perception works. You can choose how you perceive the world. With every interaction, you can make it about you or understand that people act based on their reality and perceptions and that there are always other ways of looking at things. Allowing yourself to shift your perception and have a better experience opens your world to more possibilities, leading to better results. It is your choice. Choose wisely.

Chapter 6

Living from Love

"Love is what we are born with. Fear is what we learn. The spiritual journey is the unlearning of fear and prejudices and the acceptance of love back in our hearts. Love is the essential reality and our purpose on earth. To be consciously aware of it, to experience love in ourselves and others, is the meaning of life. Meaning does not lie in things. Meaning lies in us."

— Marianne Williamson

It sounds simple to live from Love, yet it is one of the hardest things to do unless you are always spiritually aligned and connected. We are spiritual beings living a human experience in a Spiritual Universe. In our human experience, we can choose to live in love or live in fear.

When we think of living in Love, we often think of the human experience of feeling love or being in love. We think of the emotion and experience of love from a parent, friend, perhaps a spouse, and in turn, we have loved many people. That emotion may be easy to feel for a heart-centered person, yet when we become disappointed or hurt by someone we love, we can easily allow our head to govern our emotions as a defense mechanism and turn to fear-based emotions. According to acclaimed psychiatrist Elisabeth Kübler-Ross, there are only two human emotions: love and fear. All other emotions stem from these two primary feelings that cannot co-exist, so when we are in a Love state, we cannot experience fear-based emotions. Being in a state of Love engages our inner Being (heart/soul) whereas being in a state of Fear involves ego-based reactions that lead us from our head.

"Fear vanishes only with the annihilation of the ego," Mahatma Gandhi said. That statement is true because fear-based emotions are born from the ego. As Marianne Williamson said in this chapter's initial quote, ego is why we learn fear. As a baby, we did not have an ego. The ego is created as we develop our conscious self. Just like we can shift our perception of the things and people in our outside world, we can shift our emotions from head-centered to heart-centered, from fear-based to love-based. By taking on this practice of living from Love, we shred our ego. It is not easy. That is why it is considered growth.

A Mother's Fear Molds a Daughter's Behavior

I grew up in a patriarchal family, but my father was often gone, working up to three jobs to support us—his five children and wife. His time at home was limited, and when he was home, he was often sleeping due to his exhausting work schedule. That meant that by default, my mother was the decision-maker in the home when it came to the children's activities. My mother clearly loved her children and wanted to keep us safe, so she made decisions out of fear and did not allow us to expand our world. Unconsciously, she leaned on fear and guilt to control and maintain order in the home. When I asked my mother if I could partake in after-school activities or go on a sleep-over at a friend's home, or anything other than my normal routine, she said, "No, because if something were to happen to you, I will have to answer to your father," or "Okay, but be careful because if something happens to you, I will have to answer to your father." Those words echoed in the depths of my subconscious as a child and into adulthood. It made me sensibly scrutinize my decisions and actions. As a child, my common thought was, *I don't want to get my mom in trouble with my dad.* I trusted that "something unpleasant" would happen if I failed to do as she said, challenged her decision, or acted rashly. I did not understand at the time that those words were meant to "keep us safe" through guilt.

Based on my mother's behavior, my interpretation of the world was that it was unsafe to do and enjoy activities away from home, and to this day, I battle with a fear of travel and new places. My decision-making was also plagued with the anxiety of "something could go wrong," and my ability to interact with the world was stunted. In picking a college, I had the opportunity to spread my wings and explore a new world. I really wanted to go to a college thirty miles from home, yet despite my desire, I chose to attend the state university in my hometown. Thirty miles is not far, yet to me, at times it felt like I was going away to another continent.

My mother's fear paradigm led me to believe the world around me was not safe, but the natural desire for growth led me to a spiritual connection with God and to trust in Infinite Intelligence. The transformation has not been easy, but it has allowed me to turn the page and live from Love.

As a parent, I can challenge the old paradigms and encourage my two children to live from Love. When my son was ten and wanted to hike the Grand Canyon with his Scout troop, I hesitated because of the possible danger, yet I asked, "Is that what you would love?" His excitement, resolve, and desire for the adventure ahead led me to consent. When my daughter's college choice was 330 miles away from home, I supported her. Time and time again, I have learned that acting from "What would you love?" draws an expansive result that enriches all concerned.

God Is Love

"We know how much God loves us, and we have put our trust in his love. God is love, and all who live in love live in God, and God lives in them."

— 1 John 4:16

Living in love is a spiritual devotion that aligns you with the Laws of the Universe; God, the Infinite Intelligence, gifts you with breath each moment of each day. God is the source of unconditional love. At times, you may have felt that love. It is unlike any other. You may not be aware you have experienced God's love because it is in everything you see and do. When you go into nature and become part of the tapestry of creation, you become one with God. When you sit on a park bench and look to the horizon as the sun is setting, you encounter the divinity and wholeness of the Universe.

When you are in your backyard watering your plants and feel the air on your face, simultaneously smelling the sweetness of honeysuckle; when you encounter the gaze of a young child and sense the wonder and innocence of their soul; when you are in the stop and go of the morning commute and beyond the clouds you discover the formation of a rainbow; when you wake up every morning and sense the newness of the day, the opportunities ahead, and the beauty of the interactions with loved ones, then you can realize God's love is everywhere and all the time. You just need to be awake to see it and appreciate it.

Here is where many of us miss the miracle of the moment and the unconditional love that God has for us. God's love is not dramatic. It is subtle, soft, kind, generous, compassionate, joyful, grateful, content, and a host of positive emotions that give us Life.

God's love is visible when we are filled with joyful exuberance because of some wonderful thing that happened. It is easy to be grateful in those moments. But what about when life is challenging and difficult? It is much more difficult to be love-filled and grateful under duress. This is where our thinking must be challenged and our perspective changed. In the most challenging moments, if we can demonstrate gratitude by controlling our perception, we have an opportunity to learn, to find answers, and to receive the gift. As classic self-help author Napoleon Hill said, "Every adversity, every failure, every heartbreak, carries with it the seed of an equal or greater benefit."

Living from love at the most trying times is the answer to overcoming with grace and flow. When we surrender and let go and let God, we transform our energy and we are given a higher awareness. Letting go and letting God means to submit and trust that there is a higher purpose in the situation. As a person on a human journey, we may not understand the reason for the undesired circumstance. As Reverend Dick Gregory said, "Fear and God do not occupy the same space." Therefore, by trusting God, we are casting away the fear our human side may want to lean on.

Reframing the situation from a bird's eye view perception can ease the setback. For example, suppose you get a flat tire on your way to work; what is your go-to reaction? You have a choice on how to react. You can be mad, disappointed, or frustrated. Or you can be curious with self-talk like, "I wonder what this flat is preventing me from experiencing" or "What will this new experience bring into my life?" Then, while you are waiting for road service to arrive, you hear about a major accident by your work and realize had you not gotten the flat, you would have been at the intersection at the time of the accident. You then have the answer to why you got a flat tire. Looking for the bird's eye view of a situation allows you to see there is a larger picture to the circumstance. You switch focus from the problem and see the experience as something to learn from, something more expansive than the immediate situation.

You won't have an immediate answer in every situation, but trusting and knowing there is an answer will lead to gratitude, and in due course, things will be revealed to you. Being grateful for every event, no matter the perception of that event, good or bad, is living from love. Seeing the goodness by flipping the perceived bad to "There is a greater benefit in this situation" takes rigor, but when practiced and nurtured, it can become innate. This one habit can change your life and help you see the love unfolding in your life. This is living from the inside out. Living from the inside out means living from what you are intentionally seeing and feeling, instead of the circumstances apparent in the outside world. You are dictating your response to the conditions of the outside world; the condition is not dictating your reaction. When you perceive the event or condition as a page in your book of life and see it is filled with God's love, you know it is a gift filled with golden nuggets, and you can expect goodness to reveal itself.

The Golden Rule

Most faith traditions observe the Golden Rule, "Love your neighbor as yourself" (Matthew 22:39). In Buddhism, the rule is expressed as, "Hurt not others in ways that you yourself would find hurtful,"

(Udana-Varga 5:18). In the Abrahamic religions, it is "Love your neighbor as yourself," (Judaism; Leviticus 19:18), "Do to others what you would have them do to you," (Christianity; Matthew 7:12) and "As you would have people do to you, do to them; and what you dislike to be done to you, don't do to them," (Islam; Kitab al-Kafi). Most of us believe in this rule, yet we may find it difficult to practice in some circumstances.

The Golden Rule is easy to follow when other people behave. But as we know, we can't control others' behavior. We can only influence our own behavior, so that is where we start. When we were children and someone was upsetting us, we learned to defend ourselves and react according to the situation. And that was appropriate behavior for children learning to navigate and experiment with life. As an adult, we can challenge some negative behaviors directed at us through methods that conform to spiritual actions. What if we behaved differently? Would the outcome be different? A friend of mine tested the theory and found astonishing results.

Experimenting With the Energy of Love

Paul was taught when you respond with love, the situation, no matter how tense, can be transformed. He was resolute about testing this idea and got the opportunity one day when his neighbor, Sam, came to him with an issue. Sam's voice was loud, his tone was accusatory, and his gestures threatening. The anger and emotion Sam projected toward Paul were pronounced and seemed poised to escalate to a dangerous level. For a moment, Paul believed it might not be the appropriate time to test the theory since his neighbor might get physical with him. Despite all the signs of danger and the possibility of physical harm, Paul decided in a split second to respond to Sam with love.

Paul allowed Sam to yell at him as Paul directed "I love you" thoughts to his neighbor. Paul chose not to speak, yell, or move toward Sam—he just stood with his entire being sending love, feeling love, and being love to his neighbor. Paul's love muted Sam's offensive words.

The scene went on for a few minutes, until Sam eventually saw it was futile. Paul was not going to engage in the hostile encounter. Sam may have seen Paul's reaction as unreasonable or disproportionate to the force he was exuding, yet he must have concluded if Paul was not going to react, continuing was fruitless. Sam then turned around, made a "Ah, forget it" gesture and walked away.

When Paul tells this story to his friends, he says he still can't believe how effective "I love you" can be in any situation. If in this situation, where his neighbor was almost out of control, taken over by his emotion, love was the tool that diffused the situation, then those words can be used in any encounter.

When you are confronted with behavior like that exhibited by Sam, you have two choices: react in kind or with love. Paul opted not to say anything. Instead, he stood there projecting the energy of love toward his neighbor. Everyone has that same choice. When you can turn a heated situation into a loving situation, you are moving in the direction of Love, living from love.

My friend Melanie shared a similar experience where she was incredibly surprised by how using love helped her manage an emotional conversation with her brother, Frank. Their father had died the day before, and they were at their parents' home helping their mother with the funeral arrangements. It was not an easy time because the death was sudden and their grief was overwhelming. No arrangements had been made in advance, making the day even more difficult.

Melanie told me the event is a bit foggy in her memory, but she remembers she found strength in a place she did not know existed. She was surprised by her reaction and is proud of herself for seeing the situation from a bird's eye view as it was happening.

In the late morning, Melanie proposed a different cremation service than the one Frank had found; he had been doing the research up until then. Frank became inexplicably angry and started yelling at her. Frank's reaction was upsetting and surprising since they had been exchanging ideas and supporting each other and their mother all day.

Melanie was troubled and disturbed, but she knew, for the sake of their mother, it was not the time to get into a family quarrel, nor was there a good reason to argue the point. Melanie chose to act and react with love, to respond to Frank with love, without judgment, and with compassion and kindness. She understood he was in pain and that what they were going through was taking an emotional toll on him, so he acted out.

Melanie ignored the yelling and simply responded in a soft voice. At the same time, she thought about his hurt and sent him all her love. Frank continued to yell and say things he didn't mean. He seemed to be trying to get Melanie to react in anger. She continued to talk calmly despite his raised voice. She said later "something" inside her knew his deep hurt was causing this reaction.

Melanie thought about how Frank had been so close to their dad as a little boy, and as an adult, he had always been there for every decision and every time their father needed help. She knew they were very close. In fact, Frank was telling her exactly that: "I know exactly how Dad would want his funeral because I was his son; we had deep conversations. I was always there for him."

Melanie knew attacking or defending would only escalate the situation, so she stood down despite Frank's attacks. Because she saw the little boy inside him, she could not attack the fifty-year-old man.

Frank's tirade continued for some time. At one point their mother intervened, telling Frank, "I don't understand what is going on. Melanie, you, and I all want the same thing—to bury your dad in peace." After that, Frank continued his attack for a few minutes, but eventually, he saw the futility or just ran out of steam. Frank saw Melanie was going to remain a loving and caring sister. He drew back, calmed down, and lowered his voice.

Afterward, they just moved on as if nothing had happened. Weeks later, when Frank came to Melanie to apologize for his behavior, she simply said, "I love you, and I know it was a tough time for all of us."

These two examples are not unique. You may have experienced something similar, or you can recall situations when you could have acted or reacted similarly. These stories demonstrate what an extraordinary vehicle love is. It can turn the worst events into good experiences, or at least mitigate profoundly painful situations. When you chose to act from love, to see love, and to be love, you are growing in awareness and consciously acting in accordance with the Golden Rule.

After reading 1 Corinthians 13:4-5, I see how Paul and Melanie's actions were an act of love. Corinthians says, "Love is patient, love is kind. It does not envy, it does not boast, it is not proud. It does not dishonor others, it is not self-seeking, it is not easily angered, it keeps no record of wrongs." Paul and Melanie's actions would not be easy to maintain if their intention were not based on having a harmonious relationship with the other person. Despite what the other person said and did, they maintained their love and loving posture, and both view those events as extraordinary. They tell their story as an example, not as a boast. They were surprised by their actions and how effective acting from love was. They have both expressed how those experiences changed them. They continue to live from love. They may not be perfect at it, but seeing the result of their actions inspires them to continue to strive for loving results in their relationships.

Self-Love

"You, yourself, as much as anybody in the entire universe, deserve your love and affection," the Buddha said. A core teaching of Buddhism is self-love because it is believed that once you know how to love yourself, that love will extend to others.

It is difficult to love yourself if you are self-critical and expect more of yourself than you do of others. Think of a situation in which you blamed yourself for whatever went wrong or where you thought you could have done better. If you think of that same situation but see your best friend as the actor, you will likely excuse your friend's behavior. You will likely find logical reasons for the behavior or find compassion for your friend because, after all, your friend has been through a lot. You protect the ones you love and accept them with their faults. To love yourself, show yourself the same compassion.

Self-love also means being our own best friend and making our happiness and wellbeing primary, doing for ourselves "what we would love" in every situation. As social creatures, we evolved to please others to win approval. This was necessary to our survival. We still have the instinct to disregard our needs and wants to please others. But we are also self-aware. We can rise above instinct and live authentically in the purpose our Higher Power gave us. We must consider our needs and do the things that make us happy to be whole and aligned with Spirit. When we are aligned with Spirit, our mental and physical health thrive.

Loving ourselves means owning ourselves, being free of the "what will people say" recording in our head, owning our actions, and being true to who we are in every way, despite the flaws others may see. Remember, we are our biggest critics, and while we are concentrating on our flaws, others are concentrating on their own flaws. We are not the main character in other people's lives. When we offer to ourselves the same grace we offer others, we shine.

You are a wonderful human, full of gifts to offer the world. Infinite Intelligence supports you and love lives inside of you. You love others. You see beauty in others. Take the time to see it in yourself. Once you take off the critical glasses, your light can shine brightly. Your radiancy shines through confidently once you accept yourself for who you are and cherish what you have to offer. Stepping out to be your authentic self may seem courageous when you lack self-acceptance. But it is no more courageous than loving your best friend. It is innate.

Self-love begins by reining in self-doubt. Every person has their own self-made reality. That reality is their perception of the world, so shifting perceptions brings change. See yourself as a spiritual being living a human experience with successes and failures, just like everyone else. You are loved beyond measure by Infinite Intelligence, who lives in you to support your dreams. Magic happens when you love yourself completely—a new world opens. We find self-compassion in knowing each person is special in their own journey. There is no comparison because everyone walks through life in their own way. Understanding this idea leads to inner confidence. This confidence allows you to step out and be you, without judgment or criticism, with compassion and self-love.

Self-love takes practice, but the more you do it, the more comfortable you become with you. You discover your gifts and share them with others. You experience deeper relationships since you are living from your true source of love. You understand that who you are reflects your beliefs and perspective. When you are living from love, joy, and gratitude, you see love, joy, and gratitude in the world. Self-love is accepting your magnificence and clearly, lovingly accepting everyone else because you are at peace with who you are.

You are now living from love and feeling at ease with the world. That discovery leads to a dance with life. As Oscar Wilde put it, "To love oneself is the beginning of a life-long romance."

Love Heals

Gary Zukav, spiritual teacher and author of *The Seat of the Soul*, said, "Eventually, you will come to understand that love heals everything, and love is all there is." I agree. Think of the times you were upset, disappointed, or hurt and, in that moment, a child gave you a hug, or you just saw them smile. You felt your energy shift and the negative feelings dissipated, if only for the moment, yes? It is difficult to fight against love. I'm not sure what time heals, but I believe love heals all wounds. Nothing is more powerful than love. Love always wins, no matter what the circumstance may be.

Heal Thyself

Patrick Snow, my publishing coach, shared a strategy he uses when cycling. Patrick is in his fifties and enjoys sports like skiing and bicycling. He loves to cycle around the islands of Hawaii and enjoy the beauty of nature as he gets closer to Source, God. Patrick said when his knees hurt from strenuous cycling, he concentrates on God's unconditional love focused on the physical pain. After deep concentration, he feels warmth in the area and the pain begins to dissolve. Being able to infuse God's unconditional love with his body is a great gift that allows Patrick to continue his physical adventures and live life to the fullest.

While I was undergoing treatments for breast cancer, I used to heal myself mentally. It was one of the most powerful tools I used to avoid the side effects of sixteen rounds of chemotherapy and thirty sessions of radiation. I believe it allowed me to heal from the surgery with ease. For example, radiation treatments tend to cause dry, cracked skin and fatigue. Radiation zaps your energy. Knowing radiation can be an energy sapper and cause sunburn-like damage to the skin, I used the power of my mind to redirect the radiation's energy. While I was receiving the treatment, I imagined God's unconditional love beaming on and healing the area, bypassing the skin, and going directly to the areas that would benefit from its loving energy. I also imagined it filling my body with energy, not depleting it. It was remarkable how visualizing healing energy worked to keep the treated area from breaking and my body from getting tired. I also did not experience any of the other side effects like nausea.

In addition to envisioning radiation therapy transforming into love energy, I told my body, "I love you," and "Thank you" every chance I got and religiously while showering. I have replaced thinking about the day's to-do list or what happened the day before as I shower with the ritual of thanking every cell in my body for the wonderful job it is doing in producing vibrant, energetic, and dynamic health.

Findings That Support Theory

Your body and everything, whether living or not, responds to love because everything is energy, and infusing and directing loving energy into things produces positive effects.

Japanese scientist Masaru Emoto did an experiment in the 1990s where he studied how labeling containers of water with different messages affected the crystals formed in frozen water. For example, writing the word "love" on a container of water led to beautiful crystals, while a message of "hate" caused the crystals to be deformed. In his *New York Times* bestselling book *The Hidden Messages in Water*, Emoto detailed his study supporting the idea that human consciousness can change the molecular structure of water. Other people have performed the same study using rice as the object, and the methods discovered by the study are today used in horticulture as a means of growing healthy, thriving plants.

It is also evident that love is an energetic vibration that can be felt by people and changes the energy in the places surrounding the vibration. If you have ever been in the company of someone who practices being love, coming from love, or simply living a spiritual life deeply connected to God, Infinite Intelligence, then you have experienced being in the presence of Love, and you know it is an immensely powerful energetic field of reverence.

You have the power to generate love energy. All you have to do is think it. Think you are love; think you act as love. You can respond on behalf of love in any situation and transmute negative energy into a positive experience.

Exercise A

Form a mantra that will lead you to live from Love.

1. If you practice daily affirmations or would like to start the practice of transforming yourself, consider affirming as often as you can throughout the day. Recite the following:

    a. I am love.

    b. I am loving.

    c. I am loved.

    d. I am love in every action I take.

    e. I am the presence of love.

2. Reminding yourself of these truths daily—when you get up in the morning, as you are getting dressed, when you are driving, when you are cooking, when you are walking, as you enter a room, when you meet someone, etc.—will bring about a shift in your energy. You will be welcomed with smiles, and your presence will change the energy in the rooms you walk into.

Summary

"When you find love, you will find yourself.
When you have the knowledge of love, you will
then feel peace in your heart. Stop searching
here and there; the Jewels are inside you. This,
my friends, is the holy meaning of love."

— Rumi

Part of discovering who you are is living from the love infused in your being. You are made of Love, and it can never leave you. Rumi said, "Your task is not to seek for love, but merely to seek and find all the barriers within yourself that you have built against it." It is normal to mask your true essence—love—as a defense mechanism prompted by fear-based thinking. It is not easy to shed that part of yourself, and it's a lifelong journey to live in the present, embodying loving thoughts, feelings, emotions, and actions.

Recalling your true essence of love and feeling empowered to enjoy life for all it is constitutes a growth journey well worth the time and effort. Once you start that journey, it is difficult to turn back because you become enveloped in an infectious life-giving energy. It is a journey that turns all negativity and suffering into light, a light that shines through you no matter what you are experiencing. It is like regaining focus and going back to yourself. It begins to feel like the natural way of being since it is who you are.

I challenge you to live from Love, to embody love, be love, offer love, emanate love, and act from love; in return, you will live abundantly. You will be living in a state of consciousness whose vibrational frequency attracts only love and abundance.

Chapter 7

Turning to Mercy

"Blessed are the merciful, for they will be shown mercy."

— Jesus Christ

What is mercy? Mercy is a broad term referring to forgiveness, benevolence, compassion, and kindness. It is used in the many religions around the world. I love the word because it cloaks you with forgiveness and helps you be kind. When you think of being merciful, you are already in an energy beyond the offense and embodying love in the actions you take.

Knowing how energy works lets us remember others' actions are not about us. In *A Course in Miracles* it says, "I have said you have two emotions, love and fear." And as we discovered in the last chapter, fear is a reaction to a threat, something new, something different, something we have not experienced before. As spiritual beings, we are born to love, to live from love; we are love, so when we are the victim of someone's offense, the love we have for that person is overshadowed by fear. At the human level, we may have good reason to fear them, to be cautious and act carefully when dealing with them. But that fear should not affect our life in a negative way. It should not turn into hate, disgust, or vengeance. Allowing others' actions to affect us so dramatically would rob us of part of our peace. Allowing it to happen is a choice.

Holding On to Hurt

When Evelyn married her high school sweetheart, she thought the marriage would last forever. She even consulted a tarot card reader who affirmed her belief. Evelyn was fifteen when she met Jack. Jack was a handsome young man who loved women, cars, and taking care of his good looks. Evelyn knew Jack was a flirt, but despite warnings from her mom, sisters, and friends, she wanted to spend the rest of her life with him. She thought he would change and eventually settle down with her. After high school, they went their separate ways until a few years later when Jack was visiting his family. During their encounter, Evelyn became pregnant. Jack felt trapped, but he was committed to being part of the baby's life.

Jack, Evelyn, and the baby became a family. Evelyn was happy because her dream to be Jack's life-partner had become a reality. Jack knew he had settled, but love for his child and his sense of responsibility helped him accept the situation. He was attracted to Evelyn and knew she was deeply in love with him, so he believed he would eventually come to love her.

After a couple of years, Jack and Evelyn had a second child, bought a house, flourished as a couple, and eventually married. Jack was content since it was apparent they complemented each other as a couple. They accumulated financial wealth, enjoyed good health, took annual vacations, and had affluent friends, fancy toys, and nice cars, yet something was missing—they did not have real, passionate love. Because Evelyn didn't feel loved, she became insecure in their marriage. Jack's charm continued to catch the attention of other women. Although he was not physically unfaithful, he did not properly respect his marriage and continued to flirt, joke with, and smile at women he felt attracted to. His behavior caused disharmony in their marriage.

Evelyn's insecurity haunted her with thoughts of losing her marriage. Her insecurity led to distrust, and eventually, her social drinking turned into a drinking problem. Jack had no intention of leaving his marriage, especially since the kids were in high school and he thought it would hurt them. Evelyn's drinking escalated, and she was verbally abusive to him in social settings. It was embarrassing, yet he remained committed to the marriage until it became unbearable for him and the kids.

The family planned an intervention. They recorded Evelyn in one of her drunken tantrums to inspire her to seek help. It did not work, and Jack saw his life unravel with insurmountable pain and unhappiness. Not only was his marriage unhappy, but Evelyn was an abusive drunk and had no intention of changing or seeking help. Jack had to make a decision—to be happy, he would have to upset their world. It was not easy to end the marriage he had committed to long ago.

During the divorce, Evelyn became even angrier, not only at Jack but at anyone who was part of his life—his family, his friends, and his coworkers. It was as though she was asking everyone who loved them both to take a side. It was war. Jack, on the other hand, was free to be himself. It was as though he was breathing different air and could fully enjoy life. He had to restart part of his life. He called it a fresh start and infused it with the intention to be happy. Evelyn was a good person, he cared for her, he respected her as the mother of his kids, as the woman who stood with him while they built financial stability, and he wished her well despite her actions.

Although Evelyn tried to use the kids as pawns to build a wedge between their father and them, the kids were old enough to know the truth. They navigated this time cautiously, not mentioning their dad to their mom or acknowledging that they remained close to him. It was a sad time for all of them.

Anyone who knew Evelyn felt her pain and despair; she had lost the love of her life. She had destroyed their family, although she would never see it that way. From her perspective, Jack divorced her to be free of her and the kids. It was a very awkward time for everyone who loved her as she dealt with her alcoholism, broken marriage, and anger at life. She had never imagined ending up alone.

After their divorce, Jack and Evelyn both had other relationships. Jack remarried and had a happy marriage that changed his flirty behavior. His wife is secure in their marriage, has a great relationship with his children, and after many years, has developed a courteous relationship with Evelyn. Jack continues to wish his ex-wife well, and they even see each other at their kids' functions. He has moved on, embracing his new life and his new wife.

On the other hand, Evelyn remains bitter and has not moved on from feeling the pain and suffering of her marriage. She is recovering from her alcohol addiction. She has had romantic relationships, but her partners end up as enemies, and she remains single. She says she does not want to get married again because it is too painful and she is not meant to be married. She is holding on to the fear and hurt of her experience, which continues to rule her life. She has a lot of resentment toward her ex-husband and continues to blame him for her unhappiness and for taking away her dream of being married forever.

A Shared Experience

Anyone who has been married or spent time with a married couple understands marriage is an everyday decision to share your life, embrace the other person as they are, grow, and support one another. Within a marriage, you may, at times, experience hurt feelings, disagreements, and offenses that leave long-term effects. This is true of all relationships, and to maintain the relationship, you have to forgive and let go, choosing to move forward and not hold on to the past.

Evelyn and Jack's story demonstrates how choosing mercy frees the person showing compassion and forgiveness and releases the energy to move forward. By moving forward, you have an opportunity for a redo. You have a chance to choose happiness, joy, and love. You can learn from the circumstances that hurt you to make better choices in the future and grow from the experience. Turning to mercy and being forgiving, compassionate, and kind can shift the direction of your life. Mercy is the only real way to move forward, move beyond, get unstuck, free yourself from a prison constructed by your own mind, and grow.

What if you decide to or have already forgiven someone? What thoughts, feelings, and emotions would you or did you experience? Were you worried, with self-talk along the lines of thinking they will cause you more pain or they are "getting away" with something, thinking they will not learn anything?

Remember, turning to mercy is not about the other person. It is about you. When you act mercifully, you are staying grounded in your energy; you are keeping your power; you are living in the flow. It is a gift you give yourself.

Holding on to negative thoughts and emotions imprisons us in constrictive energy. As soon as we release them and let go, we free ourselves from the pain of the offense. We no longer carry the load of the injury, hurt, and suffering. We realize forgiveness is easy when we find compassion for the person and for ourselves. We learn to separate the person from the offense. The person hurt us, but they continue to be the same person we once trusted. Had it not been for this circumstance, we would still be in harmony with them. We realize the person was acting from their own fears, protecting themselves, and at the time of the offense, they were not capable of acting from love.

Acting from fear is a human reaction that can be transformed when you have the awareness to respond from love and not react from fear, when you realize acting from ego leads to more pain and discomfort. It is painful to hold on to the anguish of being hurt and uncomfortable to act against your loving, authentic self. When you hold a grudge and allow someone else's action to alter your peace, you have lost your inner power. Don't give up your power, your peace. When you live from love and move in an expansive flow of energy, you can see the offenses against you as evidence of fear in another. Your perspective changes, and you shift your response to compassion, which can lead to transforming the other person's energy into love as well.

How do you not react when someone is attacking you or hurting you? The first step to changing your reaction is to know you have a choice—you control your response. You control your thoughts, feelings, and actions and can pause your actions. You do not need to react immediately. The lull between action and reaction, or better, between action and response, is a calming force that allows you to respond from your higher self, your love center, your heart.

The lull gives you time to remember things happen with you, not to you, and they are powerless unless you give them energy. Shakespeare wrote, "For there is nothing either good or bad but thinking makes it so." Circumstances, conditions, and situations are neutral until you provide the energy to act on them, until you decide they are bad.

Discover your ability to pause by taking a breath. It takes but a second to decide what your response will be. It can all be good if you choose. It may be difficult to overcome ego at first. Ego has guided your perception of situations and made them about you for a long time. It will take practice, awareness, and concentration to form the new habit of following love and ignoring ego.

Seeking a Higher Self

Will is a client who was on an intentional path of self-discovery and growth. His spiritual teacher introduced him to the Vibrational Scale of Consciousness, so he decided to stay in tune with the frequency he was living in and adjust and calibrate what he was feeling to choose a higher frequency. If he was feeling guilt, shame, or pride, he knew he needed to look at the situation differently to change his feeling and lean on trust, acceptance, and love. He was deeply committed to staying aware and working with his teacher to understand and practice shifting the frequency of his vibration.

One of the first adjustments Will worked on was changing his feelings about religion. He had grown up in a deeply religious, Catholic family and been forced to attend church and Catholic school. As an adult, he felt guilty for not living up to the expectations of his family and the church. He looked down on people who practiced their faith publicly, attending and praising in public, yet leading what he felt were hypocritical, dishonest lives. Will remembered family conflict, even right after church, that didn't seem to follow the church's teachings. His experience left him with the perception that religion did not serve anyone. He was a good person; he did not need religion to tell him how to live. This mindset led to feeling anger, fear, and guilt, so he decided to work with his teacher to change his perspective.

With his teacher, Will successfully reframed his view of religion and God. He understood his perception was based on what he had learned as a child. He was committed and continued reframing his ideas and letting go of the negative paradigms, making a choice to take on the work that changed his perception and helped him have a better relationship with religion and God.

Although Will made great strides in changing his perspective on God and people who professed their religious beliefs publicly, he couldn't totally internalize the idea of compassion and grace for everyone, even those who didn't seem to need or deserve it. The idea that deserving has nothing to do with grace is a big concept, and it takes constant practice to stay in grace. When you are compassionate, you do not measure whether the person is deserving of compassion or how compassionate you should be. Mercy is not tied to the person who may have committed the offensive act; it is the action taken by the person called to act in grace toward the other. You can be merciful even when the other person has no regret for or feels no guilt over their actions. You can be merciful even when the other person continues to offend. This is when you have the capacity to turn to mercy and evolve the feeling into love.

When We Are Ready

We are all at our own distinct level of awareness, so we can't all shift our mindset so we respond instead of reacting. It is a step-by-step process that we can only successfully undertake if we have compassion for ourselves. As French theologian and philosopher Pierre Teilhard de Chardin said, "We are spiritual beings living a human experience." In our human journey, we are learning and practicing different principles and moving up a spiral of awareness. The beauty of the human journey lies in our ability to continue to grow and learn. Therefore, we are called to be patient and compassionate with ourselves. We will learn the lesson when we are meant to learn it.

When Eckhart Tolle's *The Power of Now* was published twenty-five years ago, everyone was saying it was a must read. At that time, much like now, I was on a quest to be better, to act better. In seeking growth, I read several self-help books about our higher consciousness. I bought a copy of *The Power of Now* and was extremely excited to start reading. I reserved a weekend to get started, but to my dismay, the book was all Greek to me. I did not get what Tolle wrote. It was frustrating. I continued reading, trying to understand, but I just didn't. I put down the book for a while and then tried again. I did this several times before I gave up. I eventually gave the unread book to a secondhand bookstore.

A few years later, when I had studied and practiced more, I found a copy in a bookstore, picked it up, read a bit, and to my surprise, I understood what I was reading. I was elated not only by finally being able to read and understand the book, but more importantly, because I then understood the concept of "level of awareness." I understood I had to grow spiritually to comprehend what was being taught. Understanding this concept made me more excited about learning, and I let my intuition guide my selection of what to learn next.

In that moment, I also shed my shame/guilt about reading "New Age" books. Since I had grown up Catholic, I felt seeking answers outside the church led to being judged harshly for learning and believing the concepts of Spirituality. I also understood why people would not understand and would judge my choice to evolve my beliefs. I was okay with being different, thinking differently, and having different beliefs. I was free to be myself without fearing criticism since I knew the setpoint of our beliefs is related to our spiritual consciousness.

It is easier to be compassionate toward someone when you know we are all doing the best we can from our belief setpoint. You can be compassionate with yourself instead of blaming or judging yourself when you know you are evolving and growing and that the experiences of today are the foundation to the person you will become tomorrow.

The Birth of Compassion

Will had difficulty turning judgment of unjust situations into compassion for the unjust because it is a difficult concept. His feelings came from love, loving people, and wanting the best for others; therefore, he was stuck on how to respond to the mistreatment and infliction of pain with compassion for the person inflicting the pain. He was also bothered by how judgmental he was being. He wanted the anger and judgment to stop but did not know how.

The lessons Will learned about turning judgment into compassion did not resonate because he did not consider the responsibility that comes with such awareness. When we are aware that we are responsible for our own emotional state and our judgments, we realize we are also alone responsible for our mental state, reactions, and actions. When we offer compassion for those who do not deserve it (which is everyone, us included), we are really freeing ourselves from their injustice or wrong actions. We do not condone their actions; we cannot change their actions. If we give them power in our mind, we only cause ourselves pain. When we have compassion and grace, we free ourselves of their actions—they can no longer control us.

Then, we find contentment in leaving behind expectations we place on others' behavior and become aware that being judgmental has no effect on them. When we come to this realization, we can be at peace with the situation—it's not that it is okay or we are neutral on the subject, but we can see the situation for what it is—an act of fear. We don't let someone else's behavior dictate our actions or state of mind. The world's problems no longer have power over our feelings, emotions, responses, and reality.

Nurturing Yourself

The Buddha said, "If your compassion does not include yourself, it is not complete." Self-compassion is a challenge. You are toughest on yourself. What you expect of yourself is usually much more than what you expect of others. Self-love and self-compassion are overlooked when you live in your head. Your thoughts tend toward judgment and blame. You put yourself down for being too fat, too short, too talkative, or not good enough. You can easily be compassionate with a friend who makes a mistake, encouraging them with kind, uplifting words. But that is not a conversation you have with yourself.

It takes some work to get the voice in your head to say, "I know you didn't mean to do that," or "I love you," or "Everything is going to be okay," or any number of other comforting words like we find so easy to come by when comforting a friend. But this practice is essential to undertaking spiritual growth.

When we falter, we tend to hold on to the offense and beat ourselves up about it. It is important to practice acknowledging we did not behave as we would have preferred or that we made a bad choice in handling a situation. Acknowledgment is important in understanding we have room to grow and then doing the work to grow, moving on and doing better the next time. Learning and letting go instead of replaying the failure in your head is an important step.

Don't waste energy on what you do not want—shift to thinking about what you do want.

Showing yourself compassion is knowing that if you could have done better when you faltered, you would have. You always have a level of awareness, and as you grow, your awareness expands. Perhaps if you had not made the misstep you are judging yourself for, you would not have had the experience and raised your awareness. Knowing Infinite Intelligence is involved in everything that happens is part of spiritual forgiveness. It does not mean you have free rein to falter, but when you do, the best action to take is understanding it, picking up the lesson, and moving on.

Release shame, judgment, and guilt. The lower frequency of those emotions will not heal your wounds or anyone you may have hurt. They will only continue to hurt you. It is easy to point the finger and judge. Doing the work to heal is rigorous.

Healing starts with yourself because as you heal, you stop carrying the shadow of the past, the burden of the offense; you separate the offense from who you are as a person. It is like a reunification of the self with the self. In self-judgment, you are separated into two parts: the one that judges and the one that feels judged. By being compassionate with yourself, you melt and fuse the energy to align with one force—self-love. Love for yourself is the beginning of love for others.

Taking on this practice does not mean you deny reality. You are acknowledging the facts and setting them in front of you to learn from. You set an intention to do better in the future, be compassionate with yourself and your actions, and love yourself for learning and wanting to do better. It is a process. It takes practice. The more you engage in this ritual of self-forgiveness, the clearer you become about who you are and how you want to show up in the world. This method leads to self-understanding and self-growth, and it nurtures the soil of conscious living, of self-awareness.

Exercise A

1. Recall a situation where you feel someone acted wrongfully toward you.
2. Recall a time when you and that person were in a different situation, an enjoyable or pleasurable event when you felt goodness from that person. If you do not have a memory of this, reflect on a time when you saw them in a different light than being an offender.
3. Think of their actions not as directed toward you, but only as actions that happened. Bring compassion into your thoughts using all or some of the statements below, or make up compassionate statements that feel good to you as a healing thought.

a. "I have so much compassion for the person who [name the wrongful act]."

b. "I feel compassion for them because they know it was a wrongful act, and they wish they could have done better."

c. "I have compassion for [name of person]'s actions because [the act] demonstrated their fear. They are a loving person."

d. "[Name] was acting out of fear, and the actions were not about me, but about how they were feeling. I have compassion for them because they were afraid."

e. Make up your own statement to bring healing to the situation.

4. Separate the offending actions of the person, from the person; know that those actions are not the person. Know they are a loving person and are not just their actions.

5. Think of a person you love unconditionally (your child, parent, spouse, best friend), and feel the deep and loving feeling you have toward this person.

6. Engulf your entire being in the love this person makes you feel, and then think of the person who offended you.

7. Continue to do numbers two to six as many times as needed, eventually only doing number six as a daily routine until you feel a shift in your energy when you think about the offender.

8. If the offender knows of the offense and has asked for your for-
    giveness, reach out to them, and tell them you forgive them.
    Closing the circle brings finality to the situation so you no longer
    play it in your head. Remember, in this step, you are forgiving
    the person, not the offense. The behavior was not acceptable.
    You are not normalizing it by forgiving. If you think it necessary,
    say so when offering forgiveness to the offender.

9. Send a wave of love and forgiveness to the offender energetical-
    ly when the offense creeps into your mind.

10. Continue to work on compassion and forgiveness for the offense
    for as long as it takes; depending on the length of the script in
    your head, the exercise may require months of repetition.

The exercise above takes rigor, commitment, and desire for change.
It requires you to want to change the energy that envelopes your
body when you think of the offender.

You may think of a person you feel judgment toward, yet you are
unable to remember why or recall a specific incident. This may be
related to something you see as a character flaw in them that has
nothing to do with you but still brings you to judge them. For these
cases, you can do steps five through seven, and nine and ten.

Exercise B

Forgiveness is a daily ritual, just like bathing and brushing our teeth. Life happens daily, and we may face conditions and events that require us to ask a daily question, "What do I need to forgive today?"

Ask daily, and acknowledge an event that transformed your energy and requires your forgiveness. Some examples of daily events where you feel a constrictive energy are:

- A person cuts you off in traffic.
- Your boss puts more on your plate without acknowledging how hard you have been working.
- You don't honor yourself by taking time to refuel and recharge at lunch and just eat at your desk.
- The person next door does not respond when you greet them, and you feel ignored.
- A person you love and expect time from overlooks your need.
- You allow guilt, shame, or worry to hijack your attention.
- You feel anger or judgment toward another.

After asking yourself, "What do I need to forgive today?" and coming up with a situation, move your energy to nonjudgment, compassion, and forgiveness. Commit to not overthinking the situation but simply making it a forgiveness practice that releases you to live a happier life.

Summary

This chapter was about liberating yourself to a higher conscious to allow yourself to climb a ladder of awareness where you live life's moments with love. It was about challenging you to make your practices similar to taking a daily shower to discard the grime your body holds. You can do this by practicing the daily release of energies that hold you down. Live lighter because hatred, judgment, regret, shame, and other similar emotions imprison you and keep you from living freely. Commit to growing from the experiences you are living, taking responsibility for your actions, and living a much freer, fuller, expanding life.

When you realize that every person's actions derive from their level of awareness and understanding, and you have no control over them, you comprehend you can only control your reaction. You are here to learn how to respond to the situations in your life. Working to be a better you is the only thing you can do. Take on the work of non-judgment, compassion, and forgiveness and you will lead yourself to experiencing the freedom of looking at the world through the spectacles of love. You can transform your experiences into the golden nuggets you learn from, and you can notice your advancement in conscious understanding that you are here to refine yourself into being a better being.

Mary Morrissey says, "The content of your life is the curriculum of your evolution." When you understand that everything you experience is for the purpose of growth, it becomes easier to understand life is not happening to you; it is happening through you. You are then in control and can see others' actions as a means for your growth.

When you are offended, you can look at the offense as an opportunity to grow yourself and practice compassion, non-judgment, and forgiveness. This is a daily practice. You will be challenged in this regard, but as you continue the practice, your challenges will become smaller, and your expansion will be greater.

The energy of an angry, sad, and fearful person is dense, dark, and feels almost as if the air is being sucked out of the room. The energy feels very constrictive. But when you are in the presence of someone living a joyous, loving, caring, and compassionate life, the energy is quite the opposite, feeling weightless. It is an expansive energy. Rather than participating in the energy field of negativity, you can shift the energy by blessings and mentally sending love to transform the energy. You can be the vehicle of love in a place of darkness and stand in the light of pure unconditional love.

> *"A person experiences life as something separated from the rest—a kind of optical delusion of consciousness. Our task must be to free ourselves from self-this imposed prison, and through compassion, to find the reality of Oneness."*
>
> *— Albert Einstein*

Chapter 8

Releasing Resistance

"The intensity of the pain depends on the degree
of resistance to the present moment."

— Eckhart Tolle

W hen you shift from judgment to compassion, you move your energy into understanding the circumstance the other person is facing, not the hurt you may have felt. Releasing resistance works in the same way; it is about shifting your struggle energy into one of peace. Motivational speaker Tony Robbins says, "Energy flows where the attention goes." In other words, simply by putting attention on the unwanted situation, you create more of what you do not want.

As part of our human journey, we will experience hardships and events that cause us pain. We are conditioned to resist certain things because we do not want them in our life. These situations may be divorce, bankruptcy, betrayal, death of a loved one, or a diagnosis, yet we are called to face the circumstance because it will not go away. At such times, it is wise to welcome the release of resistance and accept that we are in our *Dark Night of the Soul.* Accepting the situation will release energy that mounts when we resist—energy that blinds us to the answers and actions that can help the situation. Just like judgment and resentment jail, resistance creates a struggle that is impossible to get away from.

You may have experienced or witnessed a relationship involving infatuation. Two people mutually like each other, but one person's feelings grow, and those feelings are not reciprocated. The person who holds greater feelings wants a deeper relationship; they seek more harmony and unity the more they see their beloved. They want to spend more time with them and love them. However, the person whose feelings have not grown would rather spend less time with or not see the other; they begin to feel discomfort because they feel they are being chased. The other's feelings and actions seem overwhelming and unnatural to them. The more the person feels chased, the less they want the person. Meanwhile, the person in love is holding on to that love so tightly it is all they focus on. They are caught in a circle of emotions they can't escape, and when they are rejected, they crave the other person even more. They are unable to see beyond themselves and how, ironically, the more they hold on, the more the other person rejects them. Once they let go, the energy erupts into a harmony of normalcy. The analogy of a child throwing a tantrum over a piece of candy they see at the grocery store comes to mind. Once the child is taken away from the candy aisle and can no longer see the candy, a calming release of force happens. It is the peace of acceptance.

It takes rigor and practice to release resistance. Curiosity is a good resource to turn to in this practice. By becoming curious about the situation, you can move the focus from you or the event to wonder and creativity. The flow of energy is no longer a struggle. It becomes a search for answers. You are no longer holding yourself hostage in suffering, but you are reaching out to the universe for answers. Being curious about why you are feeling this way, and what is emerging in the situation you face allows you to interact with the situation. You are no longer being controlled or manipulated. You are allowing the Infinite to take the wheel to lead the way while your inner guidance knows all is well. You are in the hands of God. As you allow this energy to come in, an inner peace and resoluteness guides your body, mind, and spirit. This is the beautiful experience of knowing you are one with spirit and the vehicle through which life lives.

Staying curious opens the space for answers to come through. The gift of wonder replaces the anxiety of control. You begin to see the opportunity in the situation and understand you do not have the answers. A greater power is acting in your life that looks to provide for your greater good. In your human journey, you tend to think you can control the situation. You recognize that the situation is not what you want, and you do all you can to get it out of your life. You believe you can resist and overcome, yet often letting go and letting God is the only response that makes sense. You begin to comprehend this when you realize that when you try to control the situation, it tends to get worse—it feels like you are hitting your head against a brick wall.

Your observer self begins to see patterns in the situations you try to control and only make worse, so it leads you to try something different by letting go. You see a relationship you should have let go of sooner or you realize you held on to that crappy job for far too long. You see that by holding on instead of letting go, you have been causing more damage to your finances, health, or relationships, or you realize the manipulation you use on loved ones is a disservice to who you are or are endeavoring to be. Letting life unfold instead of trying to control it begins to make sense as a practice.

To have these epiphanies, you must be awake at the helm of your life, not on autopilot. When life is happening to you, the opportunity for learning and growing is diminished. The beauty of life is that it is an experiment—a classroom to learn in where you can allow life to happen *through* you. When we are in those moments when we think we can control it, life provides feedback by making the situation more difficult, prolonged, and arduous. At times, we don't let go until disaster happens, manifesting illness, broken relationships, or other difficult life situations. If we do not listen, the feedback gets louder and less friendly until we listen, or it becomes too painful to ignore.

Demonstrations of Everyday Life

You've had a situation where you want something to happen, so you start forcing the idea or situation in the direction you want it to go, but then the resistant energy becomes palpable. Finally, when you let it go, the opportunity is there. An example we can all relate to is when you misplace something like your keys or a pair of glasses. You look everywhere for them, searching every nook and cranny in your home for where you could have left them. Then, you finally give up looking; suddenly, you see them in a place you already searched. How could you have missed them? You were holding so tightly to the energy of finding them, of them being lost, but when you released the lost energy by stopping your search, you became open to knowing they were somewhere (not lost), and that is when you spotted them.

Releasing to Life's Unfolding

My friend and colleague Mary told me about a day when everything she did turned out differently than she preferred. She and her husband were trying to get pregnant. They were scheduling baby-making time with her monthly ovulation cycles, and this particular month, she felt especially confident she was pregnant. People around her were telling her she glowed. She was full of joy and had a sense of completeness. She interpreted her feelings as a successful start to a new life. She felt very connected to her husband, enjoying the journey in their marriage and becoming parents. She was at ease with her work and felt she was living her dream. Her relationship with her parents was great and got even better with the expectation of a new baby in the family.

As the day progressed, the energy shifted, and Mary felt the signs of her monthly cycle; she knew that once again they were not pregnant. In her work-life, she felt like she was behind, not prepared for the next workshop. She also felt disconnected from her husband because their plans were not coming to fruition fast enough. She realized her mom and dad felt a disruption in their plans when she announced she might be pregnant. As she focused on the day's tasks, she noticed how her energy felt depleted, how she sensed she was not good enough. She did not feel worthy of living the life she had dreamed of. Then she felt tired in her body, mind, and spirit. The question she posed to herself was: How did today feel so different from yesterday? As she paused to see the why in the question, she saw her feeling centered on what she wanted. Since she wanted to be a mom again, to be pregnant, and while she thought she had reached her desire, she felt successful, she was on top of the world, yet as soon as she discovered she was not pregnant, it all crumbled. All the feelings of fear, abandonment, discouragement, and an unfulfilled life were suddenly present all at once.

Wow! What a gift that realization was. Mary's shift in perception from happily pregnant to another false alarm made all the difference in the circumstances she thought she was living. When she thought she was pregnant, she felt great, and life was working out. But when she found she was not pregnant, her reality changed. That awareness helped her understand the importance of letting go, of releasing life to unfold in its own time.

Mary later told me how living through that experience was such a gift in her journey, how she was able to see the pressure she was putting on herself and her relationships by wanting to be pregnant so desperately. She said once she let go of the desire to be a mom with an open hand, leaving it up to Spirit to work in her life, she felt such relief. She knew her desire to be pregnant and have a child had not changed, and that it would happen in its own time. Then I asked her, "What if it doesn't?" She said, "Then I know that it is not to be, and motherhood will manifest in its own time, in its own way."

A few months later, Mary was pregnant, and as she navigated her experiences, she had a different understanding of how to release and let go. By letting go and turning to Spirit to assist with the manifestation of your desires, you can live in flow with life.

The Desire for a Job

David found himself laid off at the age of fifty-three for the second time. He came from a generation that was taught to stay in a job—to be loyal to the company where you work for a lifetime. Despite his desire to work and serve a corporation for as long as he could, he found himself facing another layoff due to reorganization. He had worked for the first company for twenty years. He started at entry level and moved up the chain as a smart, articulate, confident, and loyal employee, yet he was dismissed regardless of his contributions. In the second company, he commanded the same values and strong work ethic, once again thinking it was the company he would retire from. Then he discovered they had also decided to end his employment after seven years of loyal service.

David researched new companies to work for, scouting one he felt was a perfect match for his values, skills, and dreams of finding the company he would retire from. He applied for a job that fit like a glove. He knew people in the organization and reached out for recommendations. He was surprised when his contacts did not respond, yet he continued his effort to get a job there. Eventually, he got an interview and planned to fly out for it.

In the meantime, David saw another opportunity at another company. The position also looked like a perfect fit, but he knew little about the organization. He applied for that position also because he knew better than to put all his eggs in one basket. Still, he continued to focus all his energy on the first job opportunity, seeking out contacts and preparing for the interview.

The second company also called David in for an interview, and he accepted. In this case, he didn't need to fly out because the interview was coming to him—they were considering several candidates in the area. He felt good about both interviews afterward, yet he continued to focus on the first company, thinking its reputation, history, and his connections there made it the ideal place for him.

The best-laid plans did not work out as David hoped. The first company called thanking him for his time but saying they were going in another direction. It was a huge disappointment. He had had it all worked out in his mind. Then his thoughts began to play. *Maybe they didn't hire me because I am too old. I was the perfect fit. Why didn't they see it? How could I miss the opportunity? What did I do to turn them off? Oh, my goodness! I missed a great opening that may never come again.*

A few weeks later, David got a message from one of his contacts at the first company. His previous colleague told him he had not replied because he did not want David coming to a place he would not last. He told David how miserable he was and how he was looking for a new company.

David thanked his former colleague but thought to himself, *Well, I could make great contributions and my experience would be different. I would have been a great fit.* He discounted his colleague's comments because of his desire to be part of that organization, the organization that had not made the offer he expected. David also reminded himself other contacts in that company had not responded, and he saw them as perfect fits, just like he would have been.

David was relieved when the second company welcomed him with a job offer paying more than his previous salary. He promptly accepted the position. Looking back, he sees he has been able to grow in his career, he feels valued and supported, and he has enjoyed his time there. He is now looking forward to retiring.

David had put out resistance to all but one opportunity, setting his mind on a certain company, a certain result, and was disappointed. Now he sees the gift in what he did receive. He sees that despite thinking he knew what was best for him, a Higher Source was leading him to where he would be rewarded for his commitment and loyalty. He was supported in finding the place that would see him retire contentedly.

As David tells the story now, he views the experience with the gift of hindsight. He is ready to retire and has loved every opportunity and his time with the new company. He sees that the people he didn't hear back from at the first company had moved on within a year of him reaching out to them. He sees how their lack of communication was their way of protecting him. It is an assumption on his part, but he thinks if they had given him references, he would have received the job, and he believes, since they were not happy, he would not have been happy either.

David's plans worked out anyway. His intention to be in a company that welcomed and made use of his gifts worked, and he achieved his goal. Releasing control allowed him to live into his desires.

In Control of My Health

James is eighty-three and has always been in control of his life. When he was young, his mom died and his father became an alcoholic. James learned to fend for himself. He quit school to get a job. He got a job on a nearby ranch where the owners knew of his misfortune and helped him by offering a job working with the cattle, a place to sleep, and food. Later, James set his sights on trucking, earning an apprenticeship at sixteen—he lied about his age to get it. James was inquisitive and hardworking, and he learned various other trades—mechanic, taxi driver, and maintenance.

At twenty-three, James settled down and started a family with a young woman named Marilyn who was nineteen. Despite his lack of formal education, James worked hard and did well financially. He and Marilyn had four children, and he found creative ways of taking care of his family. His life seemed full and great paths opened when he needed them to support his growing family.

James retired at fifty-five. Their home was paid off and he and Marilyn owned another property they rented out. He spent his time connecting with his grandchildren and gardening. He spent time on home projects and caring for his fabulously maintained and manicured garden, which he loved. James was happy.

James was satisfied with how his life had evolved. His success was a product of good planning, hard work, and his commitment to making things happen. He felt controlling his circumstances was the key to his success.

When James had faced difficult times, he faced the challenges head-on and conquered. He had managed every challenge. But at sixty-five, he was diagnosed with diabetes. He controlled the disease by changing his eating habits. Then he started to exhibit age-related health symptoms like sexual dysfunction, periodontitis, and glaucoma. He was dismayed to see his body breaking down, and despite adhering to the treatments, he found little to no relief.

Frustration and dissatisfaction set in for James. His body was breaking down, and this man who once had full charge of his own life, who managed every aspect of his success, no longer had control. He had never learned how to let go. As a devout Christian, Marilyn had told him about the concept of letting go and letting God. James thought his wife left too many things to God. James was not prepared to start living and doing things differently.

Marilyn saw the challenges James faced. She loved him very much and wanted him to be happy, so she prayed for him to be able to release control and accept the changes that came with this period in life. They ended up talking about these challenges daily. She asked him to embrace their new life and be thankful for being alive. They were truly blessed, she reminded him, with a great life, great memories, loving children, and grandchildren. And their grandchildren were now having children of their own—it was such a blessing to see their great-grandkids join their family.

James listened when Marilyn repeated their life's blessings, but he was still miserable, feeling like he was less than a man. He could not allow himself to become dependent on his wife and kids. He could not face his decline and would not bend to it. Accepting it would be death to him.

James was at a fork in the road that many seniors face as they decline in vitality, health, and a desire for life. He became depressed. He hid it from his children and Marilyn and continued to work on home projects as best he could. Even the easy projects became challenging as his body aged.

This was not the life James wanted. As his sight declined, he felt his control over his own life slipping away. He could not picture himself being a burden to anyone. He saw only one way to maintain control of his life—to end it on his own terms.

Under all of life's circumstances, James had been in control, changing and evolving to face the next step in his journey. He had always been in control of his life, and that is how he ended it. He took his own life.

I believe James' decision to end his life served his purpose as a person whose biggest fear was to be dependent on his wife and children, He was a proud man who had always controlled his circumstances and could see alternatives. We will never know how life could have been different had he chosen a different path and released control as his wife suggested. The purpose of this story is to demonstrate the extent of the control we assume in our lives. We have free will and are able to act as we wish. Yet I believe with free will comes a responsibility to make choices for the highest good of all. I can't help but think how his death affected his family.

Observations

Each story above demonstrates how our humanness leads us to believe we are in control of our lives and can get our desired results by making good, logical decisions. We do affect our reality, but not in the way we think. Our reality reflects our thoughts, ideas, feelings, and actions as they are co-created with Infinite Intelligence. We can direct life to happen in a certain way by living from our point of power, which offers much better results. Interacting with Spirit and following its guidance and the whispers of God's voice helps us along our journey.

It is not easy to look beyond our five senses. Letting go is about being more in tune with our inner voice, understanding what "is happening to us" is of our own making, and the things we resists have gems of knowledge embedded within. The seeds of our own Becoming sprout in our toughest moments—if we can just let go of control and release resistance so life can unfold for our higher good.

Our Higher Being has a bird's eye view of our journey. We are in each moment caught up in living the life of the now, publishing the chapter of our current reality, and we have no knowledge of the many chapters yet to be written in our book of life. We see life happening one way, and we think we are directing it, yet we have no insight into how the future will evolve and the lessons we are to learn. Knowing when to let go is key to living a fuller and higher expression of our lives and becoming the person germinating each moment.

Exercise A

When faced with a dilemma or condition you are trying to control:

1. Take a step back to see it is only a chapter in your life, not your whole book.

2. Make a firm decision that despite what the circumstance you are living may look like, you will be okay. Each situation has a beginning, a middle, and an end.

3. Stay open to other possibilities, knowing that when you are focused on one thing, you filter out potential solutions and opportunities.

4. Envision the result, not how you will get there—just the result you would love.

5. Sleep on it and set the intention that things will work out.

6. Ask Spirit to reveal the answer in your sleep, as soon as you wake up, within the next week, or in the timespan you would like.

7. Let go of the reins. You can let go knowing the co-creator is in your corner.

8. Tell yourself, "Everything will work out for the highest good of all concerned," and allow yourself to envision the situation working out for the highest good of all.

9. Say in your head, *Let go and let God.*

10. The answers will be revealed if you are open to listening—they may not be the answers you think best. This is where trust and belief in a Higher Source or Spirit is required.

The more you practice giving up control, the easier it gets, and the more you will see you never really had control. The flow of life is revealed when you release resistance. Only one thing is really always happening—the perfection of life.

Summary

The *Tao Te Ching* says, "When I let go of what I am, I become what I might be. When I let go of what I have, I receive what I need." The truth is we are here to journey up a spiral of life, to evolve from where we are to where our dreams see us being and becoming. We do not know how to get there. We will require Infinite Intelligence's help to get where we are going. If it were easy, then everyone would get there in no time, but the beauty of life is the journey and the person we become in the process. Without challenges there is no growth, and without growth, we would not appreciate the person we become.

Chapter 9

Breathe In Gratitude, Breathe Out Abundance

"The universe operates through dynamic exchange…
giving and receiving are different aspects of the flow
of energy in the universe. And in our willingness to
give that which we seek, we keep the abundance of
the universe circulating in our lives."

— Deepak Chopra

When you release resistance in your daily life, you are in acceptance of what is. It does not mean you are entirely happy with what may be happening, but you become aware there is beauty in what life is offering despite what it may look like; there is always a golden nugget, be it as a lesson, growth, or awareness. As you recognize that, you become grateful for the experience and thankful for having lived it. You may have heard people say they would not have wished something on anyone, but they are grateful for having gone through it after undergoing a *Dark Night of the Soul*-type experience that transformed their lives.

Once you decide to live in acceptance, transforming to easily be in gratitude for all that is in your life becomes simple. Your awareness will be open to the beauty and wonder of life and all that is present. It is as if you are looking from a different pair of eyes. The focus is on the good in everything, and the good in everything becomes part of your reality. The more you concentrate on gratitude, the more good flows in, and the more grateful you become. It is a flow of energy circulating around you; you are breathing in gratitude and breathing out abundance. And the more abundance you receive, the more grateful you become—you live in grateful abundance.

The *Upanishads*, part of a large collection of sacred Hindu books, say, "From abundance, he scoops abundance, and still abundance remained." When we stop seeing the world from scarcity, and shift our perspective to gratitude for all that is in our life, our energy opens to how plentiful our world is. We live in an abundant world and claim it by being grateful. By flipping our perspective to seeing the abundance, we can start generating more of what we want.

Lack mentality is reinforced by an "I am not good enough" belief. This script tells us we are not good enough to have what we desire.

When we see a flashy car, can we see ourselves driving it? If we cannot envision owning such a car, or house, or career, or whatever—all the things we desire—we are subconsciously thinking we do not deserve them. We only see owning what is possible in our current reality, what we can afford today. This is a self-imposed upper limit of receiving. It is where our comfort level is, and it reflects what we have, what we have done, and what we have earned. It becomes difficult to think of having more, earning more, and deserving more. We experience an upper-limit reality that is not in alignment with Source, God. When we allow ourselves to be in a constant (as much as we can) state of gratitude for what we have, we connect with Source and abundance flows into our life. We still face the upper-limit issue, yet because we relate to Source, we are able to take in more, see ourselves deserving more, and eventually push the upper-limit beyond where we are now. We experience growth.

Being in a state of grateful abundance is calming. It is the remedy for the woes and ailments of life. Once you experience it, you know you are connected to the Source of life. You have the inner knowledge that you are part of the constellations, here to live exactly what you are living through, and the experience is there to pave the way to a greater existence. You see the difficulties in your life as chapters in your book and recognize that by living those chapters, more is revealed, and you will be better off in the end. Napoleon Hill said, "Every adversity, every failure, every heartbreak, carries with it the seed of an equal or greater benefit." You know that at the end of adversity, there is a gift, a reward, a win, a lesson, or a transformation.

It can be difficult to tune into a gratitude and abundance vibration. It is easy to relate to being envious. When you are feeling envious, you do not like the feeling, but you can't help yourself. You know it's not a good feeling because its energy is contractive and comes from lack. You lack what they have. And you can also relate to feeling joyful and grateful for someone's win. You can choose to live expansively or contractively along your journey. Oprah Winfrey said, "Be thankful for what you have; you'll end up having more. If you concentrate on what you do not have, you will never, ever have enough."

This principle is very much like the "Energy flows where the attention goes" idea we discussed. When you pay attention to lack, that is what you will attract. When you concentrate on abundance by being grateful, you receive more abundance.

My Health Journey

I am immensely grateful I learned and practiced the principles I teach as a life coach before I was diagnosed with breast cancer. By navigating life based on these tenets, I had an incredible health journey. My experience was much different than the norm; it showed you can have a cancer diagnosis and still have joy, fun, love, and an expansive, life-giving experience.

I focused on gratitude for all I had, including the illness. I practiced energy work and envisioning daily, while receiving treatments, and I became a lover of my mind, body, and spirit. It was like the disease woke me up to a different world. I studied how others' results compared with mine, and along the way I affected patients' and caregivers' lives and viewpoints.

With the diagnosis, I was immediately curious. Although I experienced fear at times in the journey, it was not my immediate reaction. Instead, I pondered, *What will the next year in my life look like? Whom will I meet? What is this going to teach me? Whom will I be after the experience?* Because I was curious, I almost automatically accepted what I was going through. I don't remember ever thinking, *Why me? I don't deserve this,* or even *Will I die?* I went straight to wondering what it would offer, what I would learn, how I would grow—I knew I had the power to make it a life-generating and joyful time.

I made it my objective to behave differently than what is expected of cancer patients. I set the intention of identifying how a life coach would act while navigating this diagnosis and adopted that mindset. The answer was always live in gratitude and leave an impression of love and joy everywhere you go. "Learn the lessons along the way and accept the gift it's coming to give you."

Yes, I saw my cancer as a gift. That shift in perception allowed me to release fear, doubt, and lack, and concentrate on health, people, love, and most of all, enjoy each moment. It was a sacred time; it was like a life in prayer.

I was determined to learn all about the disease. I was intrigued by the medical community's reactions, reassurance, and empathetic demeanor. It was beautiful to see the love and care they practice daily. They are trained to respond to the patient who is usually scared. I made it evident I was not the normal patient, and with compassion and curiosity, I learned what the cancer journey looked like for so many others around me. I found most were afraid. This is a normal reaction, but learning to think differently can help alleviate this fear.

In many cases, the mind goes to the worst-case scenario. It is understandable to see the illness, the side-effects, the loss of the life associated with the diagnosis and respond from fear. It is normal to concentrate on what you are experiencing, but the more attention you give it, the more of it you will encounter. It is not easy to change your thinking when your life is being affected in the most invasive way, but it can be done, must be done, to change the experience to empowerment.

Because of my training and practice, I came from abundance and gratitude, believing everything happens for my highest good, even a life-threatening illness. Rather than resist the experience, I made peace with it and became intrigued with what it brought me. I focused on the experiences, people, lessons, and opportunities.

The dark episodes I had previously lived through transformed me into a different person, so most of all, I was curious to meet the new me on the other side of the treatments. My thoughts and actions reflected a knowing that I would be well and even better off for having lived this episode. Dark chapters had bred great opportunities before, so that is what I expected this time.

If you are navigating an illness, start practicing similar thoughts and tune in to your intuition. You will see it is possible to know, deep in your heart, your life journey is perfect no matter what happens around you and through you. I focused on life giving me the best, on gratitude for everything I experienced, and on the abundance of each day. Being grateful each morning and awake to the day's experiences, I concentrated on the beauty of my experience. Some days, the symptoms would win for a while; some days, a battle inside me raged back and forth, back and forth, between feeling ill and holding thoughts of wellness and unconditional love for me and my body. When those days came, I learned to release resistance and just sit, rest, and be.

Whenever I had a medical procedure or a doctor's appointment, I concentrated on the gift of medicine, the knowledge and education going into my care, and that the caregivers loved serving patients. I set my intention to acknowledge them at every opportunity to put smiles on their faces while I was their patient. I thanked them continuously and supercharged my curiosity about everything around me. I was interested in hearing their stories—those of the caregivers, caretakers, patients, family members, and everyone around me. That curiosity kept my mind occupied and took the light off what I was experiencing. My intent was not to mask my feelings but change my focus. I learned a lot about people, their experiences, the disease, and the prescribed medicines. Learning was fun, and at times, lightening someone's day felt like a game. People feel good about being seen and having others show an interest in them. When you are in the energy of giving out love, care, and interest to others, you enjoy the journey because you see the light in their eyes and smiles on their faces.

In turn, as I focused on other people, I received a tremendous out-pouring of love and care. I was filled with so many people wishing me well, sending me cards, email, messages, gifts, and flowers, and some were in constant contact following my progress. I received messages from people who had not been in my life for years. I had a wonderful colleague who texted me thoughts of wellness and care every Monday for the entire journey and beyond. I was gifted with love from everyone—an abundance of love and care for me and those who shared my life.

The remarkable thing about hearing from so many people and receiving such kindness, love, and care was that I had not told many people I was ill. Since I believe everything is energy, including thoughts and feelings, I didn't want people feeling sorry for me. When someone feels sorry for you, the vibration of their energy is low frequency, a frequency that sends thoughts of the illness having power over you. I was opposed to being thought of as sick or weak, so when I did tell friends and family, I asked them to send healing energy when they thought of me, to think of a time when I was at my liveliest, when I was smiling, dancing, and loving life.

A few people said, "That would be now." That reassured me I was living up to my vision about how I wanted to be during this time. My intention was to be seen living a joyous journey despite the cancer. I was viewed as loving my life, and I expressed my love for the gift of life daily. Each day is a gift to be loved and honored by embracing it.

Chemotherapy is meant to kill cancer cells, but along the way, it also kills healthy cells. I chose to look at the other side of chemo—by eliminating the disease, the treatment was giving me life. I called chemo "The Golden Juice of Life." And while it was being administered, that is what I pictured moving through my body. I envisioned being covered with God's unconditional love and every cell in my body working for my highest good. I also listened to some gratitude statements I had recorded on my phone during infusion and used them when I had a challenging day.

I believe that, since everything is energy, my change in perception about chemotherapy directed the medicine to only attack the cancer cells. I hold this point of view because it answers the question of why chemotherapy did not have the detrimental effects it has on others. Yes, I had side effects but not like what I witnessed others experiencing.

I became grateful for the experience simply by changing the way I looked at cancer. I avoided constrictive descriptions and called the cancer experience "my health journey." Looking at it as a health journey changed the paradigm of how I interacted with the disease.

It changed my perspective on what was happening. I was not battling cancer. Instead, I was making my body healthy by paying attention to it. I hired a nutritionist experienced with oncology patients who helped me develop a nourishing diet to assist my body in remaining healthy and becoming stronger. Focusing on nourishing and loving my body resulted in me ending the chemotherapy with better blood count numbers than when I had started.

I smile every time I think about my wonderful chemotherapy nurse, Regina, who on the last day of treatment turned to her peers and showed them my blood work. She said, "See, this is what I mean. Her numbers are better than when she started." She confirmed once again that caring for my body and minding my thoughts was a good course of action. It made me feel I had the power in my journey.

Gratitude and abundance help you expand your viewpoint. They provide the energy to look at things differently and change your perspective about what you are facing. They open the energy flow to ideas and opportunities to be identified and acted upon for a better experience. When you shift your viewpoint to being grateful for the good and bad in your life with belief in a Higher Being, your experience will be as you intended. Viktor E. Frankl, a concentration camp survivor and the author of *Man's Search for Meaning*, said, "The one thing that you can't take away from me is the way I choose to respond to what you do to me. The last of one's freedoms is to choose one's attitude in any given circumstance." How you deal with difficult circumstances is your decision.

My health journey continues past the treatments. I am now cancer-free, yet I hold the gift that cancer came to give me with love and care. It brought me an awareness of how precious life is, how every day is a gift, and how in the journey of life we are free to manifest the experiences we want. We are empowered to live the life we would love despite what is presented to us. Each day of this chapter in my life brought an opportunity to make it a good day. Each day brought a clear choice on how I would love to continue to live my life. It is as if the cancer came to demonstrate how life is co-created—God, the Infinite Intelligence breathes us into life, and we are the creators of the reality around us. The presence of life serves as a prompt for breathing in gratitude and naturally brings abundance into our lives.

Exercise A

Experiment with practicing gratitude for seven, twenty-one, ninety days, or even better, a lifetime. Find gratitude in everything you experience. Suggestions for manifesting gratitude include:

1. Maintain a gratitude journal, writing down ten things you are

grateful for each day.

2. When you are showering or getting ready in the morning, express gratitude for your body and the work it does. Thank your organs and systems for keeping you healthy.

3. Send a wave of love and gratitude to your loved ones every day from wherever you are.

4. Stop and be thankful for each meal. Thank all the people who made it possible.

5. Thank the driver who cut you off, the not-so-friendly neighbor, or the coworker creating drama. They help you become more loving when you send them a wave of love and thanks.

6. Thank your car, computer, and furniture for helping you and making your life easier. Everything is energy, and we have evidence that things respond to the way we treat them or think of them.

7. Thank a loved one for being part of your life.

8. Thank the clerk and bagger at the grocery store for their work.

The point of this exercise is to practice gratitude in all you do. As you practice it, you will see a difference in yourself and everyone around you. You will be happier, more caring, and kinder, and you will notice a change in the way you look at life. If you are resolute in doing the practice, one day as you are driving down the road, you may notice the entire canvas of your life is brighter, fuller, and more joyful.

Summary

By being grateful, you recognize the goodness in your life, which leads to being happy and joyful, thereby improving your general wellbeing. Your body heals when you are in this receptive vibration. It is in tune with the parasympathetic part of your nervous system, which promotes healing. Gratitude's vibrational frequency is aligned with abundance. It is no wonder living from gratitude energy supported a cancer journey where I thrived, so I call myself a cancer-thriver (not a survivor).

I do not minimize the effects of people's health journeys. Instead, I am providing an illustration of how you can face the situation differently and have a better journey and outcome. Our journey is based on our perception and reflects what we think. I chose to concentrate on its gifts and opportunities, and I continue to see the offerings and the fortune of having lived the experience.

When you are dismayed, all you can see is dread, doubt, and fear, so look for the golden nugget in the sea of despair quickly because it will bring calm. Finding the good is a remedy for the woes and illness. Once you experience it, you know you are connected to your source. You know in your heart you are part of a constellation, here to live exactly what you are living through, and the experience is there to pave the way to a greater existence. As I remind my clients "In our toughest moments is where seeds of greatness are birthed to create richer, fuller lives." The state of mind and resilience we show up with most often dictates the course that our life will take. You know that at the end of the adversity lies a gift, a reward, a lesson, a transformation, a metamorphosis from who you were to who you've become.

Chapter 10

Living Your Intuitive Genius

*"The intuitive mind is a sacred gift and the
rational mind is a faithful servant."*

— Albert Einstein

What is your understanding of God? Who is God? What do you believe in? Do you think there is a Higher Source? What beliefs were you raised with? Do you still hold the same beliefs as when you were a child? If you've developed different beliefs, what prompted the shift? Are you open to evolving your beliefs and learning from and about others' beliefs and faith? Every person has beliefs that contribute to who they are and how they communicate. No matter what or who you call the breath of life, an Infinite Intelligence causes the leaves to grow on a tree, the wind to blow, the sun to shine, and you to wake up every morning. There is a force, an energy, moving and joining force in all that lives. That force is always working in our favor and communicating with us through our surroundings.

If you do not have a spiritual practice or belief and do not perceive the Infinite Intelligence as the reason every living thing exists, perhaps you have not contemplated or have dismissed seeing the world as a wondrous creation. You are so busy in everyday affairs you don't have time to contemplate such things, right? Religion and spirituality are different things. You can be one or the other, or they can coexist within you.

If you were brought up in a religious family, did you resist going to church? Your parents may have said, "God gives us so much. The least we can do is dedicate an hour." When you went to church, maybe you did not enjoy, understand, or find comfort in the ritual. Maybe the best part was the community gathering and interacting with others. You may have formed bonds with people who contributed to your religious and/or spiritual growth. That interaction allowed you to grow and evolve your beliefs and perhaps even embrace them. Or the same interactions led to the dissolution and shedding of that part of yourself. The point is that your spiritual path took you somewhere as you became an adult and made decisions for yourself.

Perhaps some part of you misses having a religious background because you feel you have nothing to base a decision about religion and/or spirituality on as an adult. You see others bond with an invisible being but can't relate. It is an odd thing to watch, yet you are curious about what it would feel like and what it would do for your life.

Your journey thus far led you here. You can see the world differently, look for signs of God speaking to you, and understand intuition as your guiding force and connection to God. For you, this may be the first experience of listening to a different perspective about the subject, or it may be something you really do not think about.

When speaking with someone, have you ever said something you had not intended to say? You and your friend are talking about an issue they are dealing with when wisdom comes out of your mouth, saying exactly what that person should hear. You see the comfort your words bring and may wonder what just happened. At first, you may think the insight was yours because, after all, it came out of your mouth. Yet when you examine it closely, you realize something interceded. You meant to say something different, yet the words you spoke were perfect and in sync with the situation. Does this make you a wise person? Or does it make you the vehicle of something great? You have greatness inside! It is God within you, speaking perfect words, feeling perfect feelings, and allowing the perfection of you to shine.

How can you make this happen more often? How can you be the vehicle of wisdom, love, joy, and gratitude more often? It is your openness to the idea and ability to welcome it that allows the energy to work within you. Yes, it is still you but with a greater awareness of self, an understanding that you are part of the One Source, and as its part, you are the Source. When you are in the image of God, you are a replica, a likeness, a representation of God. Why would you not be able to produce the wisdom and love that God produces? You are a vessel in which God always exists. It is up to you to get in touch with that part of yourself.

It is okay to reject this idea initially, and I challenge you to think about why you reject it. Is it because you were taught differently, you were brought up differently, or do you fear being that powerful? If God is within you, there is nothing to fear. You are capable of being triumphant over any circumstance, situation, or condition. Why would you believe in your condition or situation more than yourself as a spiritual being? Why would something outside you dictate what is possible for you? That thought process is flawed.

You are a luminous spiritual being living a human experience. You are Spirit, and as Spirit, you can create miracles in your life and the lives of others just by embracing love and staying grateful—and thereby acting from love and gratitude in all you do, in all you say, in all you are. Being a living source of light and harmony is a beautiful gift. As you are presented with the gift of life, you can then present it to others by leading the way with love and grace.

Various religions' Holy Scriptures teach us that God/Infinite Intelligence exists in all things, all creatures, as every living thing stems from its creation and is part of its creation. For example:

I am ever present to those who have realized me in every creature. Seeing all life as my manifestation, they are never separated from me. They worship me in the hearts of all, and all their actions proceed from me. Wherever they may live, they abide in me.

— *The Bhagavad Gita*, Hindu scripture

Abide in me as I abide in you. Just as the branch cannot bear fruit by itself unless it abides in the vine, neither can you unless you abide in me. I am the vine; you are the branches. Those who abide in me and I in them bear much fruit, because apart from me you can do nothing.

— John 15:4-5, Christian scripture

You can easily realize this manifestation in nature by observing with an open heart and mind, staying present to that which is in front of you, and quieting the voice in your head. Take a breath, feel the warmth of the sun on your body, and see the beauty of nature. Stand still and pay attention to your body. Become one with nature. (Refer to the exercise at the end of the chapter to experience your oneness.) You are part of the miracle of life along with everything else. It is an inexplicably beautiful and loved-filled sense of being. Once you take the time to observe and acknowledge it, and the more you admire it, thank it, and love it, the more it shows up brighter and more focused in your reality. It is as though the landscape of nature was retouched by the brush of God, and you see the detail and the fullness all at once.

> *"We need to find God, and he cannot be found in noise and restlessness. God is the friend of silence. See how nature—the trees, flowers, grass—grows in silence; see the stars, the moon, and the sun, how they move in silence.... We need silence to be able to touch souls."*
>
> — Mother Teresa

When you are in the silence and stillness, you experience the now of life. You are at peace and all else gets pushed to the background. It takes practice and love to stay in that moment of attentiveness honoring God by staying still within, and at the same time, all stands still outside ourselves. This is a meditative moment of wholeness and oneness at the same time. It is an inexplicable peace you can reach, experience, and welcome, being one with all and thereby being within God. The goal is to attain that awareness of Self more and more as you practice. The more you rehearse, the easier it becomes and the faster you can reach the summit. It becomes a practice that when maintained enriches your life like no other. It feeds your brain, repairs your body, and connects you to Source. This is the meditative state.

This practice is a vehicle to remain attuned to Self, the higher being of who you are. When you are tuned in to your higher voice, you can hear all the answers. You hear the answers to the unasked questions through intuition nudging you to act or do something that may seem illogical. You've had those moments when you argue with yourself because part of you wants to act while the other part says it is an insane idea. We are taught to think from our logical side and look at the results that are tangible rather than those that are intuitive, which depend on the Faith and Trust that there is a Higher Power encouraging us to see outside circumstance to reach a greater level of greatness.

Listening to your inner guide is living from the inside out; it is living from your intuitive genius, knowing that all is well. Your intuitive genius knows all—all the answers are within you. Know that every step you take will open the path more for the next step to appear and be taken. In human consciousness, this is a scary way of living. Yet when you decide to live this way, it becomes a harmonious journey of acting from your genius level of awareness. In the realm of human existence, this can be identified as living in flow. You have had experiences where everything in life is right, feels right, and looks right, so have unbreakable faith that all is well and it will be.

How is the spell of flow broken, then, if you have already experienced the harmony of living inside out? When doubt, fear, and logic start minding your business, you get caught up in this new thought not making sense, which changes the flow of energy back to what you are used to, to your familiar paradigm. Achieving longer moments of flow is the goal as you try to live into your genius.

Know you are more than what you appear. You are eternal in your connection to Infinite Source, and when you recognize your potential and live in gratitude for all you are capable of doing, being, and creating, you break the ties of insecurity and the ordinary, becoming an extraordinary being living your intuitive genius. It takes practice and baby steps, just like when you decide to go to the gym. It takes regular practice to build the spiritual muscle and connect with God. The start of your journey is in knowing that God lives within you, not outside of you. When you observe silence, it is an easier path to connecting.

Walks With Self

I have become accustomed to nature walks as a way of connecting with God, my Higher Self, my Source. Whenever I feel chaotic energy flow within me or around me, I take long walks in silence. I walk with the intention of finding the answer to the unasked question—the true question is: Why am I feeling this way? I try to see what is coming into my path that is making me scattered and my energy chaotic. I came to this practice after becoming aware of my life's ebbs and flows and how these internal tides would change when something new started. My energy lost its harmony and direction as if it were preparing itself for a new act in the play called *My Life*.

One of the most impressive and memorable walks with nature I experienced was right before being diagnosed with breast cancer. I had felt a new season starting because my energy had intensified, and I had lost the sense of flow and direction. My energy was scattered, and I felt scattered. On a Saturday morning, my husband Daniel and I took a hike on a nearby trail that leads into Mount Diablo near our home. As we walked to the trail, we noticed a pair of deer tucked underneath one of the trees. Since they were closer to the main entrance, we decided to enter from the side to avoid disturbing them. As we entered, we saw about fifteen wild turkeys enjoying a walk on the short, grassy area with ease and calmness. About twenty feet farther along the trail, also on the right side, we saw a family of ten California quail scurrying along a path toward the brush and ducking under a huge tree that had been brought down by lightning.

I was curious about all the wildlife we were seeing; this walk felt different than most walks into Mount Diablo. I looked up and saw, on the very top of a wooden telephone pole, three black birds flapping their wings and trading places as if they were dancing as they balanced on the pole. Then on the left, we saw another downed tree hanging from the cliff. The green leaves of new life were sprouting, looking upward toward the sun from the downed tree's trunk. It was a beautiful scene of renewal and new life birthed from the old. We stood in reverence of nature's miracle.

As we continued, the trail leveled. We saw three rows of horizontal barbwire held by metal posts. On the barbed wire, we saw five finches seemingly jumping and flying from one wire to another as if they were walking along with us. Even the nature sounds were in sync with their dance.

The beauty of their synchronized movement got my attention, and at that point, I became aware I was deep in conversation with nature, each being capturing my attention as it communicated with me. I was aware of being part of the celestial flow of life's intelligence, which was transmitting a message I did not comprehend at the time, yet it was beautiful and masterfully orchestrated.

Each perfect being was telling a story, as part of the whole. I was in awe of the majesty in the moment. Then Daniel pointed to the top of the mountain where the deer that had welcomed us at the start of our journey were standing, looking regal and immobile as if part of a painting. I strained my eyes to capture their image as their perfect camouflage blended with their surroundings.

We continued our hike and I wondered what the message was. I became frustrated with my inability to translate. I was being embraced by nature, loved by God, and like a foreigner in the habitat, I was speaking a different language and not understanding what I was being told. We hiked silently as I strived to connect and comprehend.

I was disappointed by my lack of comprehension. I desired enlightenment, yet it had eluded me. As we neared the end of the trail, in my mind I insisted and asked God to please help me understand. I knew it was the density and chaotic energy that had plagued me the past few days that was making it difficult for me to reach my intuitive genius. As I finished that thought and prayer, I saw a ground squirrel scurrying from left to right about twelve feet in front of me on the trail. As I followed it with my eyes, it entered a huge field about half the size of a football field. And there they were, what seemed like fifty ground squirrels peeking their heads up from their mounds. Some were standing with families of two or three as if they were meerkats staring back at me. What an incredible scene! I saw the immensity of the field and its inhabitants, and then I connected with the message of "community."

I then turned to Daniel with tears in my eyes. I explained the feelings and emotions I had experienced on the walk and my frustration over not getting the message until the very end. He held me without speaking. My interpretation at that moment was that somehow my next journey was going to be about community. At least I had an answer. I had no specifics or any idea of the changes the events in my future would bring, yet I found peace in knowing, from my human understanding, that I had "figured out" what nature was telling me. I was facing my future with community and God at my side.

I sat with the journey replaying in my head for a few days, and I knew how blessed I was to have received such a comforting message. Once again, I was reassured of my connection with the Infinite. Since my interpretation of the message was community, I knew that something life-changing was coming. We were already living through the COVID-19 pandemic and had been sheltering in place at home. My community at that time was my immediate household. What was to come was more than that, and the message gave me the faith to know whatever was coming was a gift from God. Knowing that my intention to connect with God during the hike had been heard and how it had created a beautiful dance as I walked along the path reassured me that "All will be well."

I looked up the spiritual meaning of the animals that joined me on the hike because I was interested in interpreting the message in more detail. I was astonished at how the meanings spoke about nourishing the self, building community, being grateful, staying positive, laying groundwork, and new life. In hindsight, now that I've lived a breast cancer journey I refer to as my health journey, the message was right on. It spoke of preparing for a journey. Cancer is about taking time to nourish your body and mind. It brings so much love and care from the community of friends, family, and practitioners. Remaining grateful is the key to having a better experience. Staying positive no matter what the circumstance allows you to stay committed to life and living a healthy one. The journey laid the groundwork for me to help others in their journey, and it brought a new life. I am no longer the person who had breast cancer. I am a new person in so many ways. My life has a new meaning and intention.

For years, walking with nature has brought definite messages that help me evolve as a person, and I continue to be amazed by that day, about how close I felt to God both during the hike and also while in my health journey.

Religion and Upbringing

The idea that God is outside of us leads to pleading and supplication, asking Source to help in some way from afar. Prayer is seen as an *ask*—asking for something from Source. For some, thinking God is also inside them can be a difficult paradigm to accept, understand, and observe.

I invite you to look at prayer as a more personal way of communicating with God, Infinite Intelligence, your Source. You can simply look at life as a prayer. In Thessalonians 5:16-18 (ESV) it says, "Rejoice always, pray continually, give thanks in all circumstances; for this is God's will for you in Christ Jesus." What you do, how you do it, and the spirit in which you do it indicates your pray modality. By being grateful throughout the day, enthusiastically showing up in life regardless of what is happening is the ultimate type of prayer. When you take time to appreciate the beauty of the day, the people, the conversations, the growth challenges, and everything around you, you are experiencing devotional prayer for life. Life is your religion in a sense. You worship it and embrace it as you move through it. You see it as perfection for all that it presents because experiencing it is a present.

We are called to be in relationship with God, our Source, which is a different experience for everyone. We are all unique, and our spiritual life is a reflection of ourselves, unique in every way. It is just like our other relationships—every single one is different. Our relationship with God is the same. God has a different relationship with each of us, yet it is still loving just the same.

If you do not have a spiritual or religious practice, you may have a different way of communicating and receiving the messages from Source. You may have a relationship where being in the vast beauty of nature gives you a sense of peace and love. You may have a traditional worship style at a venue that speaks to you. You may honor the values and beliefs you learned in mainstream religion. One way of communing with Source does not take away from another. There is no right or wrong in this. Your spiritual life and connection to Source is unique to you, based on how you connect best and feel when connected. Remain steadfast and unencumbered as you seek Source. You are the highest authority on what unites you with Source. Follow your compass during this adventure called life.

How you worship and communicate with Source can also be a focal point of what joins you and your family. Religion sets the scene for communal worship, which helps you identify with beliefs and values; you adopt those as your own and feel part of a church, a community. Belonging to a religious community can be such a fulfilling experience since you can count on the members of that community to support you on your journey.

It can also be a stressful and unproductive experience if what you feel does not conform with everyone else's beliefs. Navigating this territory, maintaining your spiritual path, and staying authentic to who you are can be painful in this setting. If you stray from your authentic self, you will feel the misalignment and discord within you. This is when you feel you are navigating life without light on your path as Psalm 119:105 reads: "Thy word is a lamp unto my feet and a light unto my path." Life feels unbalanced, as if you are guessing without the guiding force of your intuition—the little voice that provides direction.

The Judgment of Self

Growing up Catholic left me with a lot of self-judgment when I got divorced. I felt unworthy. I felt shame. The church taught marriage was for the rest of your life. Because of my guilt and shame over the divorce, I hated myself. Self-talk over how horrible I was for not keeping my commitment raged in my head for five years. I compared myself to others who, no matter what, kept the marriage covenant. At the same time, another part of me was relieved and felt free.

Deep in my gut (inner voice), I knew divorce was the right decision. Many signs supported my decision, such as career doors opening so

I could support my family as a single mom, my family committing to help me, and my friends offering to assist in my journey.

I was supported in taking that action, and I was provided with the means to take care of my family. It was an interesting time where I felt divided in three sections of self—the Catholic Edna who felt shame for divorcing, the logical Edna who saw the decision as a good decision for me and my daughter, and the inner Edna who felt good about the decision and saw the signs of support. These feelings of division are not unique to me.

Take Caroline; she also grew up Catholic and was committed enough to her religion to join a religious community. She loved being of service in her church community. She enjoyed worship and community for more than twenty years, yet she knew in her heart she wanted to share her life with another woman. She ended up leaving the church because she craved companionship. She had denied her longings because of what acting on them would mean to her family. She did not want to disappoint or be judged by the people she loved. She could not stand hurting her mom and family who would see her in a different light.

Deciding to leave and actually leaving took years, but Caroline finally made the move. She judged herself for both doing it and not doing it earlier. The conversations with herself were painful and destructive. It took years of therapy for her finally to come to terms with her decision. Her three aspects disputed which was the best path to follow.

Eventually, Caroline's decision to pursue a relationship guided her to greater happiness. Once in a relationship with another female, Caroline discovered she had been beating herself up for no reason because those around her loved her for who she was. Her expectation that they would judge and leave her, or be disappointed in her, was something she had made up in her head. She had put herself through unnecessary pain.

As a lesbian, Caroline continues to be Catholic and is affected by how the religion views her lifestyle, but deep down she feels a deeper connection with Source, God, because she is being authentic and following her heart, the small voice, her intuition. She has come to realize all God wants for us is to be happy in our lives while pursuing our dreams, sharing our gifts and talents, and serving others. Caroline continues to be a woman of service; she loves her life, feels true to herself, and has a good self-image. Yet at times, she has occasion to refocus her life to be accepting of herself since she stills lives in a society where her choices are judged by others.

Caroline has developed an awareness for her life and Source. She knows she is a spiritual being living a human experience. As my mentor Kirsten Welles from the Brave Thinking Institute explains it, we have two sides to ourselves: the spiritual and the human. The spiritual is our ever-present connection with Spirit, Source, Infinite Intelligence, and God, and it has no start date or end date. It lives on. And we have the human side of our nature with a birth and death date. The point of access for both is always where they intersect— the now.

Our spiritual side often leads the human side through ideas, inspiration, and dreams. We find our way in our human journey by staying connected to our Source, God. When we listen and follow our dreams, we are evolving up the spiral of life in awareness—the awareness of our Higher Source, of the existence of the One in all of us. We see how we are connected and understand that when hurting another we hurt ourselves. It is an awareness of ego and the competitive nature of humanity. In the awareness comes a decision to live less from ego and more from oneness.

For me, this understanding explains reincarnation. I think of it as the soul living forever as an entity in Self. That entity becomes human at different stages for our soul's purpose. As we walk our human journey, when we listen to the small still voice within us telling us to live our purpose, we move up the spiral of awareness. If we decide not to listen, we face circumstances bringing a curriculum that teaches us more awareness.

I had always been curious why it appears that people have different levels of awareness. Some think life is happening to them, and they react to their circumstances. Others become aware they have a say in their circumstances and understand life is happening through them and as them. We are in constant communication with life, and our thinking, feelings, and actions reflect our own creation of life. The spectrum of awareness reaches enlightenment and self-realization. As we live our human experience, we start at the beginning, evolve as reincarnated beings, and move up the spiral of consciousness and awareness. Life is our perfect teacher.

This may not be the primary Western cultural belief, but it is what I have concluded through examining my own life and seeing others grow in themselves. I find no better explanation as to why, in our perfect world, there would be such a difference in the awareness and consciousness of the people inhabiting the planet. From my own experience, I know being born into a family does not explain why some people are very evolved and others are less so. In my own family, we are all at different levels. This is an example of awareness coming from within.

God's Presence

"Coincidence is God's way of remaining anonymous," Albert Einstein said. When you look at the times when things worked out because something happened "out of the blue," do you really think it was a coincidence, or was it a manifestation of God's energy? An example of this for me was getting divorced and tripling my income within the year. You may have examples of this kind of situation yourself. This is God's way of supporting your life, your decisions, and your path as you move forward to uncomfortable places in the interest of growth.

It can be scary to make the life changes your inner voice craves, but it will continue to nudge you in the direction of the change with a longing, and your paradigm (the habits, values, and stories you are used to) want to keep you where you are. You become afraid and ask, "What if it doesn't work out?" Taking the leap to a new life brings doubt and fear. You have to choose to move ahead and follow your dream or remain in the pattern you currently live in. The question is: "Would I be okay putting my head on my pillow for the last time if this change was not part of me at the time?"

Bronnie Ware, a nurse, talked to people about their regrets when they were close to dying and wrote about the experience in her book

228 Living Your Intuitive Genius

The Top Five Regrets of the Dying. Ware found the top regret people had was not living true to themselves regardless of what was expected by others. To live true to oneself means taking chances, following your heart, listening to your inner wisdom, and living by your intuitive genius. The genius in you provides direction. The genius within connects with your purpose and your feelings, and it is authentic to who you are meant to be. The genius in you follows your dreams.

To paraphrase Mary Morrisey, "You can live your life for ninety years, or live one year ninety times." This is a choice we all have—to repeatedly live the same year honoring the paradigms that keep us safe, that keep us from doing something new, or being courageous and living the life our genius intuition is nudging us to live.

Staying connected to your intuitive genius can help you take the steps to choose to live large and lead your life with the self-love and care you deserve.

Exercise A

When I work with clients and invite them into a meditation practice, they find the following very useful to become one with Spirit.

1. As you are sitting still, become aware of your surroundings.

2. With eyes open or closed (you may start with eyes closed and then graduate to eyes open), bring your attention to the middle of your forehead (your third eye).

3. Gently bring down your attention to the tip of your nose, and in your mind, see where your nose ends.

4. You will find that you can't detect the end point, so now you can see how everything around you is part of you and you are part of it.

5. Marinate in that place.

    a. If you are in nature (as mentioned in this chapter), you can delight in the presence of the moment, being part of the tapestry and beauty of life.

    b. If you are sitting still in a quiet space, then pay attention to your breath and concentrate on your inhale and exhale. Let that rhythm become your peaceful music within.

I suggest you set a timer for yourself before entering into this practice. Otherwise, it can be easy to lose track of time.

Exercise B

Setting an intention every morning about who you are going to be that day helps you live closer to your values and purpose.

1. When performing your morning routine, add thirty seconds to reflect on who you will be for yourself and others that day.

2. Pick three qualities to work on today. This is who you will be. For instance, set an intention to be grateful, curious, and kind.

   a. You can do this exercise weekly if you wish. On Sunday, jot down the three qualities you would like to exude that week, and leave reminders for yourself on sticky notes or cards with the three words describing the qualities.

3. Review your day or week to see how you did with a kind glance (no judgment because you are a work in progress).

4. Retry working on qualities when you see it would serve you to become the person you intend to be.

5. Be grateful for the daily opportunity to practice and refine your skills in growing into the authentic you.

Summary

Wayne Dyer said, "Be aware of your infinite connection to your source. Know that you're more than an encapsulated collection of bones, blood, and organs in a skin and hair covered body." And Saint Teresa of Calcutta, also known as Mother Teresa, said, "There is only one God, and He is God to all; therefore, it is important everyone is seen as equal before a God. I've always said we would help a Hindu become a better Hindu, a Muslim become a better Muslim, a Catholic become a better Catholic."

We are one, connected with everything. Living for the raising of another without judgment of their life is the best thing we can do for ourselves. When we love and care for one another, we care for ourselves. Seeing another for the spirit they are, not the outside person we see, will allow us to have a deeper connection with everything, especially ourselves. We can live an intuitive genius life by loving ourselves, loving others, and knowing we are all part of Source. We are one.

Chapter 11

Self-Leadership

"You begin to fly when you let go of self-limiting beliefs and allow your mind and aspirations to rise to greater heights."

— Brian Tracy

W hat is self-leadership? The term appears to be a misnomer when you think about it. Of course, you are leading yourself—who else would you be leading as the actor in your life?

When we talk of self-leadership, we are talking about *effective* self-leadership. Are we doing the right things, taking the right actions to be successful? Then we question what it means to be successful. Does it mean we have more possessions, more money, more to be proud of? It becomes an interpretation of our perception of what life means.

Effective self-leadership is managing your life with the goal of achieving what makes you happy. Whether you are a good self-leader or not depends on who the examiner is, right? Your idea of happiness is not the same as others, not even when you are raised in the same family.

Each person determines the fullness of their own glass.

How can you achieve effective self-leadership? Again, it depends on the viewpoint from which you are observing the situation.

So many aspects of ourselves seek fulfillment. We strive for a great job with financial security and freedom. We search for relationships that meet our needs. We embrace or reject ways of communicating with a Higher Power. And as we pursue more and achieve more, the normal course of our human existence is to want more.

In the regular order of life, this is a normal reaction. Every living thing is seeking to grow, be more, have more, and give more, and so it is for all beings. You see it clearly in nature, in the seedlings you plant—the goal is to exist, to live, and to be. When you witness the unfolding of life in a flower, a bird, or a blade of grass, it is a sight to see; it is the breath of life that strives to become a full-grown member of its species.

You choose to dedicate time and resources to achieving your goals and dreams in all areas. And yet within, you see things that appear to be outside your existence. You see others achieving the things you wish to achieve and dismiss your chances of achieving the same things because of the paradigms you have made an agreement with. You were brought up a certain way. You were taught certain things. You adopted beliefs that dictate what you think. You have, in fact, put an upper limit on the good you will accept in your life.

Psychologist Gay Hendricks offers the idea that we have upper limit problems that hinder our transformation. It is a tendency that allows us to remain small and not grow into our fullness, into the bright light we can be to the world.

Hitting an Upper Limit

Have you ever experienced a situation when you were at an event like a family gathering, and everything was running perfectly, everyone was getting along having a good time enjoying the moment, and then a disagreement broke out? You wondered what happened. Then you found the disagreement was over something minor that somehow turned into an enormous situation that disturbed everyone. This is the result of someone reaching an upper limit on the happiness they allow into their lives. When joy and happiness threaten to overflow, they (unconsciously) disrupt the situation to break the flow of happiness.

We all have an upper limit of acceptance that manifests differently for each of us. Understand that while on your journey of self-leadership, there may be times when you do things that will deter you from reaching what you desire. If you are not aware of it, then you can't do anything about it.

For instance, you are on your way to manifesting your life partner; you are dating someone and receive all the signals that this person is the one. Everything is jiving, but then there is genuine miscommunication on a date, so the voice in your head starts telling you, "I knew it was too good to be true. What was I thinking? I'll never find love." Then you find yourself looking for ways to dissolve the relationship. It may be better to sit and think on it. Is one event a good reason to break off a relationship that was going so smoothly, or would it be better to continue discovering each other? The upper limit you may have reached is the level of happiness that so far you've been able to experience with a partner. Seeing the event as something that happens in the best of relationships, and not as the reason to end your happiness would be an appropriate reaction, yet to some, when the upper limit is at work, breaking up seems reasonable.

I Don't Want to Be Here

A short time after I divorced, a childhood friend came to visit me. He wanted to cheer me up, and we decided to take my daughter to a pumpkin patch on a Saturday afternoon. It was supposed to be a fun time with my daughter and a getaway for me to take my mind off my concerns. As we were going through a corn maze, my friend suddenly had what appeared to be a panic attack; he started to sweat and physically tremble. I asked him what was wrong, and he just said, "I have to get out of here." It seemed odd that he started to feel uncomfortable unexpectedly.

I followed him out with my daughter as he jetted to my car. As I drove out of the pumpkin patch, he started to regain his composure. I asked what it had been about.

He said, "It's just odd to me that there are so many happy families with their kids having fun. I have never seen something like that. It doesn't seem real."

Many young families were having a good time, but I did not see why that was odd. I tried to talk to him about it, but he said, "It's just something I haven't experienced before."

That situation stayed in my mind as one I never understood until I realized it was evidence of my friend's paradigm. He had been raised in the projects of San Francisco. His family life had been very troubled. His father had abused him, his siblings, and his mother. He had not grown up making memories of his parents taking him to fun places. Despite his wish to support me by spending time with my daughter and me, he was unable to stay in a place that made him so uneasy.

It seemed odd to me at the time, as it may to you, that he was so beyond his comfort that he displayed physical symptoms. The best way to understand is to remember a time when you went to a new environment; perhaps you are used to eating at family-style restaurants and then you go to dinner at a fine restaurant you feel you can't afford. Recall how you felt, how uncomfortable you were.

Hitting Your Upper Limit

Your upper limit is related to the limiting beliefs you hold, the thoughts you feel you are not worthy of having, or the limits you feel about what you can be, do, or give. These limiting beliefs come from your history, your parents, and the people you grew up around—basically, your life circumstances. You adopt the beliefs in your environment. Even when you are actively discovering and pursuing self-growth and personal improvement, you may be unaware of these beliefs and how they are limiting you. These beliefs are your norm, so you do not see them as holding you back.

You accept it as fact that things are as they appear. Your limitations are disguised in the framework of your life as something that just is. You make excuses for it and protect the belief as a value. For instance, you may believe you can't own your own home since no one in your family ever owned their home. You do not see yourself as capable of achieving that for yourself. This is why some lottery winners lose their wealth and why you gravitate toward people with similar backgrounds and in the same socio-economic circle. It is difficult to move outside what you are used to.

How unaware we are of our upper limit is fascinating. Until we become aware of our situation, we repeat our behaviors. Once we are aware and watch our lives as an interested observer, we see how our behaviors and beliefs can become obstacles. Unless we watch for them, it is difficult to see our limiting beliefs, much less how they interfere with our lives. They are even more difficult to overcome. Once we become aware of an upper limit, the work of overcoming it can start. Yet even then, limiting beliefs and behaviors can be difficult to pinpoint and overcome.

Les Brown once said, "You can't see the picture when you are in the frame." This kind of insight is helpful, and it is one reason life coaching has become popular. It takes training and a bit of distance to identify others' limiting beliefs and help repattern them. Even when you know what the limiting belief is, change is rigorous unless you adopt a new thought to replace it, and that takes time and commitment.

You can repattern by adopting new beliefs and rewriting the script you tell yourself through ready-made affirmations that counter the belief. And most importantly, know that the power that breathes into you intends to provide you with everything your heart desires. You hold the patterns of belief that can make anything possible, so it is up to you to grow your awareness of who you are now and who you would love to be, what you would love to have, do, and give.

Identifying Patterns

As a life coach, I practice staying open to what I notice about my feelings and actions. I notice when I feel contracted in my body, or fearful, or judgmental. My beliefs from being Catholic often come to the fore when I'm dealing with guilt and judgment in various forms. I have noticed my judgmental tone of voice when I've met successful, wealthy entrepreneurs. The voice in my head wondered how they achieved their success, and subconsciously, I believed they must have done it by taking advantage of others.

I noticed a pattern with my wages. I had worked hard and was earning six figures before I chose to let that go when I was laid off in the 2008 market crash. Instead of seeking a similar job, one in line with my gifts and experience, I settled for a different career for less pay. I worked my way back to earning six figures again, then opted to change careers, going to work at a non-profit that paid less. I did this three times in my career. Was it a paradigm?

I was somehow more comfortable with less income. When I was earning more, my thoughts went to the Scripture: "Blessed are the poor in spirit, for theirs is the kingdom of heaven" (Matthew 5:3). A lot of Scripture suggests the poor are closer to God. And I had a lifetime of Catholicism.

I was surprised to discover I had an aversion to financial wealth and how my subconscious had reinforced those beliefs. Once I was aware of this, I paid more attention to how I interact with money and people with money. I've worked to repattern my beliefs about money and people who have money. I remain awake to the voice in my head as I move forward. Looking back, I've observed several times when sneaky paradigms have sabotaged my earnings.

I've adopted a new outlook about money and wealthy people, understanding that wealth is a reflection of what people put into the world and how it affects others. It is used to provide comfort for those who are making a difference so they can continue to shine their light. That framework allows me to welcome more wealth into my life.

Deciding With the End in Mind

When you become intent on being aware and growing, the first step is to observe and identify where growth can occur. You can start on a journey of discovery and have a rigorous encounter with who you are. Your higher self will be the guiding light that leads you to the answers. But it is up to you to decide to do the work. The dreams in your heart will be made possible and brought forth into being by your desire to meet the person you have in your dreams as you are becoming that person.

The challenge ahead comes from whether you want to reach your dream badly enough to strive for it and breathe life into it. It is possible once you lean on Infinite Intelligence to assist you in the process. Your belief in overcoming and becoming is the fuel that will keep you focused on the end. Stephen R. Covey said, "To begin with the end in mind means to start with a clear understanding of your destination. It means to know where you're going so that you better understand where you are now and so that the steps you take are always in the right direction." Start with, "What would you love?" to be, to do, to have, to give, and to go after it. Decide to endeavor until you get to the coordinates that are the setpoint of your dream.

In your human journey, limiting beliefs have been your setpoint for what you can accomplish because you are measuring what is possible with the logical mind; the mind experiences living only from human senses. It does not account for the person in you with a powerful connection to Infinite Intelligence.

These powers separate you from the animal kingdom and allow you to master your life. As you have navigated life, you've quieted the intuitive voices or ignored them because you believe in the analytical mind. You believe what you see, and don't tune in to the self by becoming quiet enough to hear the voice within. Your human training sees that you have achieved results thus far, not understanding that they are still limited to what is possible in your mind. When you engage with the powers within, you can achieve greater results, rising to summits you can't even imagine.

You have a direct connection with Infinite Intelligence, the greater mind with all the answers that support the fulfillment of your dreams. Leading your life and being directed by the external powers fails to account for knowing you are made in the image of God, and God acts through you for the realization of who you are, who you are meant to be or what you are meant to do, create, or give.

Have you ever wondered if what you see is all there is in life? You are born, go to school, get a job, get married, work hard, have kids, retire, get old, and die. What if that is not all there is and you have an actual reason for your existence, your purpose? That is all there is for many; perhaps they never hear the calling, or they shove the knowing aside for the comfort of the known, the secure, the guarantee. The better life is not meant for them, or so they choose to think. It is an easier path to live the dreams of another (parents, spouse, kids) than to courageously listen to how you are meant to express life. I don't claim it's an easy path, but it is an authentic path.

Ask yourself: Why would Infinite Intelligence/God create a mediocre person? Is the person who does not live into their dreams less of a creation to God? You have the faculty of self-awareness that separates you from other mammals, so you have a choice in how you want to live. For any logical person, being created to live an average life does not make sense.

And yes, you may be considered successful by society's standards and still not live your dreams and purpose. As that person, you can feel the void within, knowing there is something greater for you. What is it?

God is not common or ordinary and would not create human life to be common and ordinary. God's creations are all extraordinary, one of a kind, and limitless. And that is what you are—limitless. You have no boundaries on what you can accomplish when you partner with the intelligence of God to create what you would love. The way to co-create with the Infinite, Source, God, is to apply the powerful internal powers you were given.

Tapping Into Your Genius

As a certified transformational life coach and Life Mastery Consultant, I learned and now teach about these powers. My mentors and teachers Mary Morrissey and Bob Proctor introduced me to these powers as mental faculties. When you engage your mental faculties in a certain way, you can connect with the higher mind to manifest the life you've imagined without the limitations that the non-creative logical mind expects. This is available to everyone, but staying open to the new ideas and practices in the process is essential. Your commitment, belief, faith, and expectation lead to your results.

You have six mental faculties: imagination, intuition, will, memory, reason, and perception. Let us briefly look at each one and then provide a way to use them while you are living through a rigorous condition. This is how I was able to achieve different results and experience while in my own cancer journey.

Imagination: You have imagination as a means of visualizing your dreams and feeling with detail how you can live the life you would love. Inventors use this gift to give life to the things they see in their imagination. Physicists use it to understand the universe. Albert Einstein said, "I am enough of an artist to draw freely upon my imagination. Imagination is more important than knowledge. For knowledge is limited, whereas imagination encircles the world."

Intuition: Intuition is a powerful gift. It is a sixth sense that tells you something is right or wrong. It is the "small still voice" you hear in your head, like a whisper yet so distinctive you know it is your inner guidance. It is also experienced as a feeling in your solar plexus when you meet people. It helps you decide if they are trustworthy. You use it as a compass in decision making. Yet intuition is more than the small voice guiding the way or the feeling in your tummy. It can also be heard as you ask the Infinite questions and receive answers only you understand from a billboard, a conversation with a friend, or a walk in nature.

Intuition is your navigation system that allows you to know with calm confidence that you are making the right decision and taking the right actions. Connecting to your inner guidance, you will not fail as long as you listen and act on the gut feelings and nudges that come from within. I refer to Albert Einstein again because he honored intuition when he said, "The intuitive mind is a sacred gift and the rational is a faithful servant. We have created a society that honors the servant and has forgotten the gift."

Will: Will is not the same as willpower. There is force in the actions taken when we say, "I have the willpower to do this." The feeling we get by using willpower is that extra force required for the accomplishment of what we seek. And when we change that to "I have the will to do this thing," we work from a different energy that exists where no extra force is needed. It is just the determination to get it done. You know that you will do it because you said so. When John F. Kennedy was intent on the United States getting to the moon, he asked Dr. Wernher Von Braun, "What would it take to build a rocket that could carry a man to the moon and bring him back safely?" Von Braun responded, "The will to do it."

Will is all it takes to get anything done. It means you will find a way despite obstacles or circumstances that may appear. You know that your will is empowered by the mind of God to find ways to achieve your goal. You will be given opportunities, doors will open, synchronicity will occur—your will is like a contract with God to serve the thing you are imagining as if it is already completed.

Memory: Memory is like a movie in your head about something that already happened. You hold memories and use them to reminisce. You also use memory to learn from what you have done in the past. You can use memory to form a picture of what you imagined as your dream and hold onto that movie to repeat it in your head as you imprint it in the mind of the Infinite. For many, no doubt, envisioning the results of what we are seeking is a new way of using memory.

Reason: Reason is the means you use to understand and judge what you see and think. You think thoughts and come to conclusions based on your logical mind and how you've trained it to look at the world. To use reason as a superpower is to stay awake to seeing the thoughts in your head as the thoughts you would like to have.

Have you ever had a situation when your thoughts took you down a rabbit hole and you wondered how you got there? You start thinking you are hungry because you hear your stomach growl. Then the next thought is about the food you would like to get; then you recall the restaurant you went to last week and how the server was the least attentive person you've ever experienced. Then you think about why you left a tip even though they didn't earn it. In fact, you should have asked for the manager and described the terrible experience you had. You may still be able to talk to the manager because the restaurant is close to school, so next week when you go to class, you may have the opportunity. Although that may not be possible because you have an exam, and it is going to be such a tough exam because those chapters were hard to understand, and the professor's lectures didn't make sense. Oh, goodness, you don't even know if you will get a decent grade in that class.

How did feeling hungry take you to your grades?

When you allow your thoughts free rein in your mind, you are not using reason to help think the thoughts you want to think. You want to use it to discriminate between which thoughts should hold your attention and those you should let go. When you think the thoughts you want to think, for instance positive thoughts, those will be reflected in your reality. Reason is the faculty you use to do that. You can use reason to guard against the limiting stories you tell yourself and shift your thinking to more empowering thoughts that work to create the reality you want.

Perception: Perception helps you see things differently. You know an elephant has many sides, and the part of the elephant you concentrate on is what you see. The trunk is very different from the tail, yet it is still the elephant you see. That is how perception works. This book has a chapter dedicated to perception because how you perceive your world is very important when you are seeking to heal you mind, body, and spirit.

Living Your Genius in Health

When you are diagnosed with an illness that can end your human journey, it can be devastating. It is all too human to think the worst and fall into the gloom of a life-threatening illness. But you can choose a different experience, one that will smooth out much of the pain and trauma associated with illness. You can help your body undergo the treatments with ease. Your experience is not tied to what others may have faced. The simple fact that we all have unique fingerprints, DNA, thoughts, and worldviews is evidence we can have a different experience from others. By making an agreement using *will* and the intention to produce different results, you start focusing attention on things that will make it so. You pay attention to the way you are reasoning, perceiving, and imagining your experience will end.

At the other side of the journey, will you be healthy or weak and tired? Will you look forward to the next chapter, or will you want to stop living because you have become a burden on others? How will this end for you? When you decide to embark on this journey with the end in mind, you have control, which Stephen Covey showed to be an effective way of living into your goals and dreams. It is also a way to live with the intention of overcoming the darkness. When you can imagine that at the end of the journey, you will be healthy, vibrant, energetic, and loving your life; you are creating a world in which that will come to fruition. It is as if you are dictating your desires to be well to Source.

You see yourself living the life you would love and doing the things you would have been doing before the disruption. You have young children or grandchildren, or you have plans to travel to a specific place and enjoy time with friends and family. Before the illness, you had that vision, so why would you veer off and accept something different? To get there, you imagine the life you planned—your child walking on stage to receive their diploma; you walking with your child down the aisle on their wedding day; you on a cruise ship with the love of your life; you enjoying the family vacation to the pyramids you always imagined.

You set the scene with whatever you desire to happen in your imagination with the end in mind, so you see the colors, delight in the tastes, and live the feelings you are experiencing. You are using the faculty of imagination to set the scene, and as you are living it in your mind, you are memorizing the feelings, the voices, and the scene because in the theater of your mind, you will replay this scene as a means to refocusing your energy away from the disease.

The memory of this scene will also serve as a footprint and guiding force for your desire to live, to continue your life journey, enjoying life with everyone who loves you and you love. Dictate your wishes loudly and clearly to Infinite Intelligence, describing this life you see at the end of the detour in your health journey. It is perfect to expect with faith, trust, and gratitude that the life you are living now will lead to the life you are envisioning. As a child of God, Infinite Intelligence, you are entitled to have the life you would love. God does not discriminate and give someone something different from someone else. Every person is entitled to the same full life.

Living at an Expanded Vibration

As you are living in the day-to-day business of the illness, decide to live up to your intention and understand your perception of the illness, its symptoms, and its side-effects. Your perceptions will influence your experience. You have the capacity to perceive every situation differently and use reason to help shift your mindset. You can decide to set the intention that your experience will be easy and joyful. You know and understand this is possible because you are connected to your Source. You intuitively know all things are possible when you align yourself with your Higher Source. You understand that life is a mirror of what you expect.

When you focus your attention on the joy, love, and gratitude for every minute of your life despite the circumstances, your subconscious will look for more joyful, loving things and will give you cause to be even more grateful. What you pay attention to expands, so when you set the intention of having an easy and joyful experience, it will be so. You are not living in a different reality.

You know that the procedure itself may be painful, uncomfortable, and intrusive, but the procedure is separate from your experience. The situation does not dictate how you feel and how you interact with the world. You use reason to separate the medical procedure being performed and the experience you are living.

You create your experience by the actions you take. Start with thinking of ways to make it an enjoyable experience and decide that being grateful and joyous for every interaction you have will be easy. The thought of being grateful and joyous sends signals to your conscious mind that evoke feelings and emotions that translate into joy. It is all an energetic vibration that runs through your mind and body, and you feel expanded gratitude. As you work throughout the day, you may need reminding, but as you practice this mindset, it becomes a pattern of thought and action that delivers the intention you set. You live your intuitive genius life by mastering the channeling of the gifts you were born with.

You were born with the capacity to decide to live from an expanded vibration. Your intention sets in motion your will to make it so. You will yourself into manifesting a joyful, loving, and grateful life. It is all possible for you. You discover in yourself the innate happiness of being alive. You appreciate every moment for all it brings regardless of how it is packaged. You know that the packaging can be transformed by your willingness to see your truth as something different from what is offered. Regardless of what it looks like, you love your life, you love your journey, and you manifest a reality that gives you life.

You find that by living each day this way, everyone loves being with you, they love to serve you, and they work to provide you with a better experience. There are no obstacles; you are living a life of flow. This happens when you live with the intention to bring joy, love, and gratitude to all your interactions. You experience an unbelievable energy full of love and wellbeing, and you live life with a sense of equanimity that allows you to feel free and leave all attachment behind. You no longer wonder if things will turn out okay. You know intuitively they will. You do not have to wonder or worry; you trust.

The journey described above is the one I lived while navigating cancer. It does not mean I did not have ill effects, bad days, or times when all I wanted to do was sit on the couch and just be. I experienced some side effects from the treatments and medications, yet not to the extent I witnessed in others. The interesting thing about that period is that I now remember all the beauty in it. I have to look at my journal and notes to remember the parts that were not positive. When people ask me about it, I describe it as a wonderful time when I was filled with community and love.

So many people were supporting my journey. I felt lifted by their love, well wishes, and energy. I met some incredibly giving and loving practitioners who gave of themselves daily.

Many of my medical practitioners, including my oncologist, recognized my journey was not common. I filled their cup as they filled mine while they were treating me. They observed how attitude can smooth the voyage by revealing more positivity and optimism. They have seen firsthand that they can't suggest or nudge patients into a more positive journey since each person chooses their experience.

Each person is the highest authority in their own life, and they can only see what their paradigm allows.

It is up to you to find your way, to choose the path that speaks to you, and to set your intention on following the vision you see ahead for you. You alone can make yourself aware that even with the disease, you still have a choice—you still have control. The appearance of losing control comes from feeling you don't have a choice.

Your control lies in how you handle and submit to the treatments. You can see them as positive or negative; you can be in flow or be in resistance. What if you choose to think about the invisible good that can come out of the situation? You can shift the focus to the good things in your life, despite the circumstance you face. You see a beautiful life full of people, things, and situations that are presented to you because of your choice. Ralph Waldo Emerson eloquently said, "What we seek we shall find; what we flee from flees from us."

Everything Is Energy

When it comes to self-leadership, the important thing to remember is everything is energy. Albert Einstein said, "Everything is energy and that is all there is to it. Match the frequency of the reality you want, and you cannot help but get that reality."

It is as simple as that; therefore, when you are wanting a certain result, all you have to do is imagine the result you would love, put yourself in the result, memorize the energy of the result, and then match the energy you memorized. It does take rigor to do so since your circumstances dictate something different than what you are loving to receive. It is a daily process, and it requires your willingness to maintain the energy day after day. A helpful tool in the process is practicing setting an intention each day about who you will be that day. When you are determined and set the intention daily, reminding yourself about the end in mind, it becomes an easier mountain to climb.

Stephen Covey said, "Begin with the end in mind." Getting into this habit will level up your life tremendously, and at the same time, allow you to observe self-leadership as a focus in your life. You will develop the muscle needed to live intentionally. You are, in fact, setting the course of your life toward the destination you will love. You are not living by chance or default any longer. You are taking the helm, designing and creating your life.

Exercise A

Becoming aware of where we are and where we want to be is the first step to self-leadership. If you don't pay attention and realize a gap exists between who you are and whom you would love to be, then it's difficult to forge a destination.

1. Use the meditation in Exercise A from Chapter 10 to be still and tune into the different areas in your life—your health, relationships, vocation, and freedom with time and money.

2. Journal around where you are in each of those areas to identify if there is a gap between the life you are living and the one you would love.

3. Which area is calling you to change? In which area do you have the most discontent?

4. Journal with the end in mind for this area in your life.

5. You now have a destination of where you would love to be.

6. Keeping in mind your destination, ask yourself, "Am I willing to do what it takes to transform my life to a life I would love?"

7. As the leader of your own Becoming, who do you have to be to reach your destination?

8. What steps can you identify that will have to be taken? For example:

a. In health: Do you have to start eating better and being more active?

b. In relationships: Do you have to forgive someone, or stay open to finding the love of your life?

c. For vocation: Are you happy with the way you are using your gifts in the world, or do you require a change of direction?

d. Freedom with time and money: Are you seeking more time with family, or more money to do the things you would love?

Once you become committed, God Source will work behind the scenes to put you in the right place at the right time and open the opportunities for growth and the fruition of your dreams.

9. Make a decision and say, "I am committed to taking the steps to endeavor down the path of making my end destination my reality."

10. Write down what you see in your destination as if you were there, right now. Whom are you with? What are you doing? How are you feeling? Engage your imagination to produce a movie in your head of the life you see yourself living. (Do not pay atten-

tion to fear, the voice in your head, or the naysayers who may not believe in you. If you've imagined it, it is possible.)

11. On a daily basis, connect with your dream. A good time to do this is at meditation or when you are taking your daily walk. As you connect with your dream/vision/goal, ask the Spirit within you, "What one step can I take to move forward?"

12. Stay open to hear directions as you move in your day as well; there may be an idea that pops in, or a person who says something, or a billboard that speaks to you.

13. As you start hearing steps in your head, start moving in that direction.

You are at the helm of your life, leading your life and heading to a destination for the life you would love. Stay committed. The exercises in this book will help you stay on course. Remember that staying consistent to your image and the steps you take builds cadence and flow. This energy is required along with the burning desire for your dream to provide Spirit the coordinates of your destination. Life will support you in ways you cannot imagine. Your belief and expectation of it happening is required as well, so trust that you are supported.

"If one advances confidently in the direction of his
dreams, and endeavors to live the life which he has
imagined, he will meet with a success unexpected in
common hours. He will put some things behind, will
pass an invisible boundary; new, universal, and more
liberal lawsmwill begin to establish themselves around
and within him; or the old laws be expanded, and interpreted in his favor in a more liberal sense, and he will
live with the license of a higher order of beings."

— Henry David Thoreau

Side note: There is an art and science to this process. You can do
it independently and intently with discipline and conviction. Some
people do require a coach who can help them. If you would like support, I would be honored to support you. My contact information is
available in the back of this book, or you can seek a transformational
coach in your area.

Summary

Napoleon Hill said, "First comes thought, then organization of that
thought into ideas and plans, then transformation of those plans into

reality. The beginning, as you will observe, is in our imagination."

To know what you would love, you must imagine it first. Your imagination is the bridge between the now and the reality you seek. If you can see it in your imagination, it is possible to live it. You will need to keep on course. No matter how it looks in real time, you have the ability to transform your life using your mental faculties: imagination is the leader that will make your future vison happen; will is what will give you the determination to pursue your vision; reason will tell you when you are not on track and give you the ideas to pivot back to your course; memory will show you your destination as you remember your vision; intuition is the compass that helps you determine the next step; and perception is the instrument that helps you see things as your truth.

You are the genius of your life and the highest authority on how you are to live it. Why not choose to live it in the experiment of seeing how far you can go? As my teacher Mary Morrissey said, "The content of your life is the curriculum of your evolution."

When you are living through a dark time, remember it is an episode in your life that is here to help you evolve into whom you will be next. Decide to live fully in the experiment of life, and embrace the gifts you are given.

Chapter 12

The Journey

*"The woman who follows the crowd will usually
go no further than the crowd. The woman who
walks alone is likely to find herself in places no
one has ever been before."*

— Albert Einstein

Early in life, I learned how life changes in an instant. When I was ten, my family immigrated to the United States from Guatemala and my life changed forever. The life I knew transformed into an adventure of learning and becoming acquainted with a whole new world. Although at the time I had no awareness of it, I was brought to a country that would require me to grow in ways that would never have been possible had my parents not had the wisdom to move to the US for the betterment of the family. This journey has provided awareness because of the mentors and teachers I've made welcomed. From day one, a fish in foreign waters, I learned to make the water familiar by being open to learning and the willingness to take on different personas.

As a child, I knew my culture was foreign to my surroundings, and I tailored how I interacted to my audience, even changing the language I spoke. I learned conversational English in six months, yet I was accused of being stuck up because I didn't understand the slang spoken by my peers. I learned quickly to morph my personality according to my audience.

I was born in Guatemala and grew up in a family with faithful women of God practicing Catholicism. These practices called to me from a young age, and I even considered going into religious life. Service to others was imprinted on my heart. The gift of empathy was my compass when it came to feeling others' pain. As life unfolded with its struggles, decisions, and obstacles, I looked to the church for answers, for the direction I needed. During those times, I did not find the solid answers I was looking for. I did find peace in knowing there was a divine being involved in the process in tough times, walking with me and supporting my journey. But still, in an inexplicable way, I felt alone.

It was very odd to feel so close to God, yet experience being disconnected to my Source. My God, my Source, was somewhere up in the sky and could see all and intervene. I prayed to God for help, to the saints for intercession, to Mary for guidance; it was a ritual of life to look upon my God, the Saints, and Mother Mary as supernatural beings with power over my circumstances. I knew my religious practice was not perfect, yet I felt the comfort of a wonderful, welcoming community of worshipers. It filled my heart to belong and participate. It was life-giving to share my experiences of life with others so they could take the golden nuggets and enrich their own lives. I was a devout Catholic who attended Mass daily, when possible, to be surrounded with godly love and peace.

During struggles—divorce, single motherhood, financial difficulties, layoffs—I faithfully looked for help. During the happy times—births, baptisms, financial wellness, newfound love, and marriage—I happily gave back to the church. It was a circular flow of giving and receiving grace and blessings for the faithful and devout life I was leading.

But a voice within continued to ask, "Is this all there is?" That question came up in my vocation as I felt a pull to a higher calling. I even considered a religious life for myself after my kids left home.

I had a good life, yet I was missing a vocation where I felt fulfilled. I could no longer do the mundane things because I was seeking my higher calling. I tried different professions, switched to non-profit, and still found a void needing to be filled with my true purpose. Not knowing how it would change my life, I boldly asked God for guidance. I wanted to be awakened and live my calling.

My request was for God to lead me to my purpose. To help listen for the answer, I started a meditation practice and studying *A Course in Miracles*. Answers were not easily had, despite my resolute stance on hearing them. Now I know that they had been there all along, but my denseness made it impossible to hear.

As I shared earlier in this book, one day, a handful of months after I made my request, I awoke anxious and yelled at Spirit as I was getting ready in the morning, "I need to know today—make it loud and clear so I understand. I am tired of waiting. I need to hear today."

And that very day, I discovered a career I had never heard of before: life coach. My thought was, *Do people really coach other people on how to live?* I investigated and concluded I had always been a life coach. It was something I had done naturally all my life—help others find the answers for themselves using my life as an example when appropriate.

I embarked on the journey and became a certified life coach. I share the details of this journey because it explains how Life prepares us for the next chapter of our journey. Studying for the certification introduced me to the eleven truth principles for successful living based on Raymond Holliwell's book *Working with the Law*. In my breast cancer journey, I used every one of them and much more that I detail below.

Working with the Law

Working with the Law is about living more fully as you practice the Spiritual Laws of the Universe. Applying each law in daily practices allows us to receive and give along our human journey as we connect to our Spiritual side. It is how we can choose what to make out of an experience rather than letting the experience make something out of us. Our thinking is our dominant force and provides the experiences we have. When we change our thinking, sharpen our perception, and get clear on what we want, we can achieve our goal. The force of nature is in our corner, advancing our dreams and making them our reality.

Of course, the news of breast cancer had an emotional effect on me, but had I let the negative emotions take over the situation, my journey would likely have been more difficult. As I told my oncologist, "I sailed through all the treatments with minimal discomfort because I worked with my mind."

The first step was to change how I spoke and thought about the disease. I chose to say, "I am on a health journey," and would not say, "I have cancer," because that would mean I owned the cancer, it was mine, and it was here to stay. Instead, I said, "I was diagnosed with cancer," and "I am on a health journey." By changing the way I spoke and thought about the disease, it gave me a different perspective. I was no longer powerless and gained back control.

When you say, "I have cancer," or "I suffer from cancer," you are allowing the circumstance to have you. It becomes the dominant force in your life, and it is harder to get well.

Everyone is living a health journey, whether they have been diagnosed with an illness or not. My health journey was no different. I was empowered to think of ways to keep my energy up, transmuting the side effects and controlling my health. I knew I needed help outside my family and friends because they were also on this journey with me. Their love for me would affect the way they looked at situations, so I worked with a nutritionist and a coach to help overcome some of the challenges. Anyone who wants to achieve different results avails themselves of expert help. For me this happened when it was required.

Since I was now suffering from cancer, I had the clarity to know I required help on this journey. Both the nutritionist and coach were vital to my ability to navigate this period with ease and less stress. Because they provided actions for me to take, I focused on doing the actions, taking the steps, knowing that each step brought me closer to the result I envisioned.

Nutritionally, a daily regimen of supplements and bone broth were key to supplying my body with the nutrients needed to counter the effects of the procedures. It made my recovery a lot faster and less strenuous. Yes, I felt the side effects of nausea and stomach issues, but by maintaining a healthy mindset, I overcame these effects. I used the power of thought to counter other effects, and eventually had no effects keeping me from feeding my body what it needed to recuperate.

As I reviewed my health journey and recovery, I was able to identify how I partnered with The Law to create a more giving fulfilling path while navigating a difficult health condition. Here I provide an outline of how because I worked with the Laws of the Universe, my experience was different than that of most people who face a life-threatening disease.

It was not a coincidence that I became aware of these laws before my illness. I believe Spirit allowed me to experiment with life's circumstance and truly test how each of us is capable of creating the life and experiences we desire.

Law of Thinking

This law talks about how the results we have in our lives are caused by our thinking. When we think about how things are created, they were first a thought. The predominant way we think determines the quality of our life. Being impeccable with our thoughts toward what we want will attract the thing we want. This is the practice of manifestation.

Pay attention to what you regularly think and then notice the results you are achieving.

We can't stop our thinking, but we can "stand guard at the portal of our mind" as Ralph Waldo Emerson said. When we want to achieve better results, we can choose to pay attention to our thoughts, words, and actions and shed behaviors that lead to bad results. We replace them with different thoughts, feelings, and actions.

As I previously shared, I believe my thoughts led to having breast cancer. I was not conscious of what I was thinking; it was just a fleeting thought that demonstrated my insecurity and dislike for my body image. My mind was at work every morning and every time I bought clothes, looked at myself in the mirror, passed a window, and saw my reflection. At various moments in each day, I cursed my breasts for their size and wished to be less endowed. It was a paradigm that began early and carried through my life. Something as silly as the ever-present possibility of staining my blouse as crumbs of food landed on my chest made me dislike my breasts.

I believe I manifested smaller breasts—my treatment included a partial mastectomy with a breast reduction. I no longer allow the paradigm of negative self-talk about my body. Since I've learned we can bring forth disease in our body, I no longer curse any part of it. I instead love it and thank it with a morning practice while I shower. I know the effects of thought firsthand, so I imagine a healthy, vibrant, thriving body.

What do you do when your thoughts are negative based on your circumstances? You can change your thoughts. One way of doing so is by replacing them with intentional statements that will counter those thoughts. That is what I did when I felt symptoms or negative thoughts. It is what I tell others who fear cancer will come back. Spend time forming affirmations for what you want, and when you catch your thinking and emotions floating down a negative stream, plug in the affirmation. Affirmations I still use are:

- "Every day in every way, I am better and better." — Émile Coué
- "I am healthy, vibrant, and strong; my body knows it, and shows it." — Kirsten Welles
- Every cell in my body is working for my highest good.

Life-generative thoughts birth life. Deepak Chopra said, "My every thought has the power to either wound or heal. I will use my thoughts wisely and respect their power." When your body is already undergoing trauma and is working hard to heal and overcome the illness, you can strive to help it heal by shifting your perception and choosing to love your journey, bless everything around you, and be grateful for your journey, always finding the good in everything. As you think of the good, the good expands. The illness will not disappear, but you are tilling the soil of wellness and healing so you can move through this episode with ease as quickly as possible.

Law of Supply

The Law of Supply says we are in perpetual increase, progress, and growth. We live in an infinitely abundant world. The supply is always greater than the demand. Health is abundant and disease is not normal. The thought process of *I was diagnosed with cancer*, instead of *I have cancer*, is a means of knowing I am healthy despite the diagnosis. It is a subtle thought process, but it works if we understand and know that living abundantly is living a healthy life.

I also wanted to promote a vision of health, so I decided not to tell everyone about the illness, knowing that human nature would leave most feeling sorry for me. It is in our nature to feel empathy and sympathy, and to see others in their condition or circumstance. We are trained to see the facts of the situation as truths; therefore, by not telling many people, I avoided the energy of pity. I asked the people I told to hold a vision of me in my healthiest, happiest time, to hold the memory that they have of me when I was joyous, energetic, and loving life. If they held that vision, they would, in fact, be working to see me that way again. The image of me being healthy permeated the universe as "This is how Edna is—she is healthy and loving her life." I felt that energy many times when I met with people and asked them for their healthy vision of me. I felt as if they were lifting me up.

I also lived up to that image. I woke up every morning full of love and life with deep appreciation for the day. I would meditate and see myself as healthy, vibrant, and bringing joy to the interactions of my day. Every place I went, every conversation I had, I held the smile of knowing I was alive, enjoying each moment of each day. My disposition was infectious, and as I delivered joy and gratitude to people, I received it back manyfold. By maintaining the energy of love, joy, and gratitude, I was, in fact, generating immunity, healing, and helping my body work to recover. I was helping my body do what it needed to do to be healthy.

Staying in a vibration that all is well in the present moment and not paying attention to the circumstance affects the part of your brain that works to filter what you are looking for. When you concentrate on the good, more good appears, whereas when you concentrate on the bad, you will see more of the bad. When you see the bad, you will become anxious and stressed, which actively works against healing. When you are generating thoughts of anxiety and stress, you are working against your body's healing process. Your body constricts and can't operate at its best.

Law of Attraction

Most people familiar with the Law of Attraction understand that you attract what you think, what you envision, and what you put on your vision board. And indeed, I had manifested many things in the past, including my husband, Daniel. From the very beginning of the breast cancer journey, I understood it to be an episode in my life, and that eventually I would be restored to great health. I had the burning desire for health, and I expected it. My whole being believed it, and since I acted as if I were experiencing health by staying active and engaged in life, I had no doubt I would manifest vibrant health. Therefore, it was an easy thing to manifest.

I was curious about how I had manifested cancer since I had always led a healthy life and concluded that the fleeting thought over a thirty-year span of wanting smaller breasts came to fruition. That made me question my thoughts. I understood more deeply that thoughts have power, so I consciously undertook becoming aware of them. Did part of me not want health? Did any part of me believe I would not walk away well from this condition? Did I really believe and expect to recover? I questioned because I know each of us has a part that, despite what we tell ourselves, believes or expects something different. The subconscious may hold some beliefs that sabotage our desires.

A small part of us enjoys the attention, the extra love, the being cared for, the not having to go to work part of illness. The bigger part has the burning desire and expectation of being healthy. That small part that is enjoying the love and attention can stop us from achieving the health results; that small part allows for our energy to wobble on our way to health. It is so nuanced that many are not even aware of these thoughts, yet this is what I believe leads people, despite their desire to be well, away from manifesting good health. The wobbly part interrupts our better health energy.

Along with burning desire and expectation, success comes from being aware of what you pay attention to and your actions. During the various treatments, I did not think about or expect to have side effects. I called chemotherapy the "golden juice of life" because I believed it was giving me life, not killing cells. I expected the radiation to provide me with energy and not deplete me of it; therefore, I did not have the side effects that others have. My expectation was different; therefore, my experience was different. While the treatments were taking place, I held the vision of God's unconditional love flowing through my body, and I would repeat the mantra, "Every cell in my body is working for my highest good."

Envisioning every cell in my body working for my highest good during the treatments helped me stay focused on the treatments' good effects.

In daily interactions, it was not always obvious that what I was doing was helping me, but I understood doing it differently would be detrimental to my health. I had two choices: experiment with the laws working on my behalf and feel good from the positive energy I generated with my thoughts and feelings, or allow circumstance to dictate how I felt and take the chance that the cancer would become a long, drawn-out event. I had experienced challenging times before and learned to surrender to a situation to let it teach me what it was there to teach me. If you resist it, the lesson will be painful, full of drama, and drawn-out. Having this awareness helped me stay on the course to recovery in the flow of life.

Law of Receiving

The Law of Receiving teaches us to "give" first. When we want money, we give an offering. When we want love, we are loving. When we want friendship, we become a better friend, so when we want health, we act as if we are enjoying good health.

Instead of retiring from life and honoring the illness and its effects, as much as possible, honor health. Embrace every situation and interaction by being your best self. Make choices as if you were healthy. At times, it may be difficult, yet do your best to do so. Listen to people, and provide good energy, good humor, and good perspective. Be curious about how you can serve others. Maybe you won't be able to do a lot, but you can set the intention to contribute to others.

One way I was a giver while living the cancer journey was in leaving an impression of love and care with everyone I touched. Even though some days I was not feeling well, I made no excuses when showing up for others. I continued to do the chores at home, drove myself to appointments whenever possible, prepared meals for others, and celebrated family and friends. Since we were practicing social distancing because of COVID-19, I attended virtual events. Sometimes I did not want to participate in life, but I reminded myself healthy people show up, so as a representation of health, I was also showing up.

As a life coach, prior to my diagnosis, I had scheduled training. I could have easily called the trainers and made excuses instead of showing up. I had made a volunteer commitment I kept. It was difficult to navigate at the time, but I was practicing health. When you are healthy, you keep your commitments. The second round of chemotherapy fell on a day I had training. It would have been easy to skip the morning session of the training. Instead, I made sure I had a charger with me and attended the training using my phone dialed into Zoom. It meant a lot to me to do that. I felt accomplished and celebrated by not allowing the disease to take me away from important moments.

The objective was to act as if I were healthy and capable of living my life fully. I also started writing this book during that time, and that was a welcome routine where I scheduled writing time and made life appear normal. In turn, I received loving, caring, wellness energy from people in my life, and most importantly, I received health.

Maintaining the energy to act as if I were healthy kept me focused on what I could do, not what I could not. It lifted my spirits, gave me reasons to get up in the morning, provided a sense of normalcy as I underwent medical procedures and weekly doctor's appointments, and helped me honor the health journey I was on.

I am not saying forget the illness, ignore symptoms, or live as if you are well. When my body needed rest, I honored it. I went to bed early every night, and I slept late when my body required it. It was similar to when you exercise regularly. When you first begin the practice, it is a bit tough to get into the energy of being fully awake, alive, and enjoying the exercise. After a few minutes, you actually start enjoying it and feel alive. It was the same for me when I went out for walks even though I did not feel like it. If I were healthy, I would walk for exercise, so to act healthy, I walked. I would start with a dragging feeling of, "I do not want to do this. I should be resting." After a few minutes of walking, however, I would be enjoying the wind on my face, the morning freshness, and nature. By walking, I actually had more energy throughout my day. It energized me, made me feel good about myself, and gave me a healthy perspective on how to go about my day.

The Law of Receiving is the circulation of giving and receiving. I have heard it described using the analogy of not getting heat from a woodstove until you give it some wood. And you must light the fire for it to provide the heat. Deepak Chopra said, "Giving and receiving are different expressions of the same flow of energy in the universe." They are two sides of the same coin, and to receive, the magic happens in the willingness to give.

Law of Increase

The Law of Increase is also known as praise. By praising, we raise the vibration of ourselves and those around us. Oprah Winfrey said, "The more we praise and celebrate life, the more there is to celebrate." By focusing on the good and praising the good, the good multiplies because all you see is good. Praise is an energy that expands what is being admired. Simply think of how you feel when you receive a compliment. It expands your energy and makes you want to continue to do better. It keeps you in the positive energy. It is like a fire; when you blow on it, the air makes the flames expand and glow brighter.

Because there were appointments and telephone calls, my intention was to leave the people I interacted with a sense of increase, to supply them with the energy of love and care in our conversations, to be curious about their day and wish them well, to speak words of praise and gratitude at every opportunity, and to fill their cups. The medical community give of themselves daily, and in some cases, the people they serve are at their most challenging times and may not offer the love and care, the appreciation, and the encouragement the medical care community deserves.

With insurance companies, medical offices, and receptionists, I initiated our conversations by asking about their day. It was interesting to hear the surprise in their voices when I inquired about them instead of concentrating on my needs. They are used to serving one patient after the next and receiving a thank you at the end of the conversation. The greeting at the start of a call seemed to be a surprise. It became my habit to wish them great health for themselves and family members during each call since most calls took place during the COVID-19 home lockdown. I could hear their voices change as I genuinely inquired about them and sent them energy of love and health. I believe my desire to make a difference and leave an imprint of love and care helped others during a stressful time while everyone was navigating a pandemic.

My daily alignment with praise provided me with a different perspective. I was excited about the conversations I had and loved sparking a positive reaction from people. It also generated flow since I was generous with praise and gratitude for everyone, which made me operate at a higher frequency, so that helped me navigate difficult circumstances. For example, calls about finances and setting up payments gives everyone a contracting feeling, but since I was approaching it with positivity, I found people a lot more positive and willing to help. They would extend options I had not thought of.

The Law of Increase allowed me to perceive the procedures and appointments as opportunities for better health, not as inconveniences. Whenever there were delays, mistakes, or inconveniences, I concentrated on what was good about the situation. One day, the breath calibrating machine for the radiation was not working correctly, so I had to come back for that portion of the appointment. I saw that as an opportunity to get to know the technician, learn more about the procedure, and receive tips on how best to manage the treatments. Had I not had the extra time with the technician, I may not have built the rapport that allowed her to treat me with so much care and teach me. I believe we formed a personal connection that helped her see me in a different light once I had given her grace.

Raymond Holliwell said, "When one can sing praises in the face of adversity, the adversity will soon disappear. That is not a promise; that is a Law. Learn to render praise, to be thankful for the good at hand, and you will have found the magic lamp of Spirit." This means seeing the good in the current circumstances, finding the golden nuggets of knowledge. When you are living with an illness, when you concentrate on the illness, it is difficult to move past it. It takes rigor and a burning desire for wellness to acknowledge that everything has a gem of opportunity in it. Seeing the cancer as a journey in health and learning more about how to nurture my body would not have happened during the hectic life I had been living. Spending more time with family, connecting with friends, writing a book, learning and practicing these laws, and discovering how to navigate life better are all evidence of the advantages of seeing the good in a challenging time.

Law of Compensation

This law is about seeing the abundance in your life. Like the other laws, it is about living from an expansive feeling that there is plenty of what I am looking for in the universe. When I feel a sense of lack, it is because I am thinking thoughts of lack. The premise is that you reap what you sow, so my first question was about how I reaped cancer. The thoughts about my body, my dislike of my figure, caused the disease to give me what I wanted, which was smaller breasts. To reap health, I would think, speak, and be health.

That started my practice of loving and thanking my body. In the morning while showering, my thoughts focus on reverence for the beautiful instrument I have to express my gifts in the world. I know by expressing love, kindness, compassion, and gratitude to my body, I am reaping good health.

Undergoing medical treatments with confidence, focusing on their benefits to my wellness and recovery, sometimes challenged my belief because of the effects I saw in others. I challenged those beliefs with the knowledge that their experience was not to be my experience. My God and I would walk with the disease differently because there are infinite ways things can evolve. My belief was that my experience was going to be positive and for my own good.

That positive belief readjusted my ideas about what to expect. Learning to think constructively about all people, things, events, and conditions was the key to a better experience than most have when walking with a health challenge. I trained myself to look for the good and express only goodness with my words, feelings, and actions. I built an energy of goodness around me.

This law is about becoming larger than what is in our mind, acting, being, doing, giving, serving, thinking, and simply expressing our beingness in an expanded way. It is about knowing that the power that breathes us loves to see us thrive, and by embodying wellness, prosperity, love, compassion, kindness, and positive feelings in our daily actions, we will be rewarded with the same.

Law of Non-Resistance

This law is about living in flow and not resisting the events, people, and situations that appear in your path. When living a health journey, you experience many uncomfortable situations. Your instinct is to resist. You think, *I don't want this in my life.* This thought is normal. I had the same reaction. I encourage everyone to acknowledge and feel their emotions. Non-resistance does not mean ignoring the facts. It simply means working with the energy so it can be a more giving experience. Mary Morrissey says, "It's okay to have your human experience; just don't pitch a tent there."

Once we "pitch a tent," we get stuck in the condition, making it more difficult to move away from it and into non-resistance. One way I moved forward in expansive energy was simply to become curious about what the journey would bring. Curiosity is like a vast ocean of the possibilities being welcomed into your life. When I became curious, I asked, "What will I learn?" With all the difficult times in my life, I had learned invaluable lessons that led to growth. I came out of these difficulties a different person—a person with more knowledge, wisdom, and love for life.

Seeing the experience as just another challenging situation like all the previous situations showed me I could overcome this new challenge. I knew I would overcome. It also allowed me to change my perception of the situation and how I approached it. In some previous situations, my refusal to let go of resistance delayed resolution and made them more difficult. I did not want to delay my journey to better health. I wanted to be well as soon as possible. This was the impetus behind my decision to let go and let the experience evolve.

Mother Teresa said, "I will never go to a rally against war, but if you hold a rally for peace, I'll be there." I am not against cancer; I am pro-health. I didn't make the disease my enemy. I focused on what I could do to make the experience better. In the Bible, it says to "love your enemies." Mahatma Gandhi said, "Whenever you are confronted with an opponent, conquer him with love."

How can you love cancer? My answer is the cancer came from my thoughts about my appearance, so I was not loving myself. By loving myself, the cancer would diminish. But I did not concentrate on cancer. I concentrated on health because what you resist persists, and what you put your attention on expands.

Coming to this perspective helped me manage the experience daily, bringing the same positive thought process to the procedures and daily events I faced. If I encountered unpleasant people, I met them with love, increase, praise, compassion, and understanding. My attitude turned their day around, and their attitude did not influence mine. My energy was focused on believing I was getting better. Everything I was going through was for the purpose of wellness, and my main vision was looking at the finish line with so much gratitude for being there and the experience.

Staying present in the moment, and not worrying about tomorrow helped me stay nonresistant, directing my energy toward making this moment better, making this experience unforgettable. Early in the journey, I had a CT scan and had to change into the paper pants, I found they were for someone three times my size, both length and width wise. After the scan, I asked the medical technician if I could wear the pants home. I looked very funny walking out of their facility, across the parking lot, and coming home in those huge pants. My family laughed. They saw me having fun with the process, and I created a memory. The technician also remembers me. He always smiles when we meet.

When you do not resist the situation, you are living in the moment and enjoying the life you are living. As you face difficulties, ask how you can think of the situation from a different perspective, what part of the situation brings good to you, and most importantly, what are you grateful for? This exercise will generate ideas to make the moment one you embrace, not one you resist. It was important to me that my family got the impression I was showing up for this journey as my best self. The desire to leave a good impression, to set an example for my children, and to be happy transformed how I viewed the cancer journey. I viewed the journey with love, not resistance or hate.

The Law of Forgiveness

The Law of Forgiveness is one of the most important laws when you are traversing an illness. I invite you to take a kind glance at where you tend to live at a lower frequency. What are you hating, judging, or blaming? How are you being prideful, feeling shame, or feeling guilt or anxiety? These feelings, when carried in your thoughts for a long time, create the stuck energy of disease. You are not at ease with part of yourself. For example, I was not at ease with my body, in particular my breasts, and over time, my wish for smaller breasts invited the disease into my body. It was not intentional; it was just a daily thought about my discomfort with my appearance. I was not loving and accepting myself. I desired a different appearance.

Studies of the body-mind connection continue, but it makes sense that if happy thoughts and being grateful build immunity, then disempowering thoughts will do the opposite. I have seen disease invited by a pattern of thought several times. The main premise is that everything is created twice—once in thought, then in reality. Since thoughts are energy; they create a form of energy that becomes a thing.

When you do not receive what you want, like health, you can become anxious, nervous, sad, impatient, and angry. These feelings are contractive within your body and counterproductive to healing. How can negative energy be good for healing? Let go of the negative. Acquire the sense of life's importance and free yourself of negative emotions. Then a cleansing of the held energy from darkness to light will happen, and when you are in the frontline of an illness, you need all the light and love on your side.

Understanding forgiveness was important to my journey. I examined my relationships, including my relationship with self. I asked, "If today were my last day on earth, would I be okay with the impression I left, the mark I made, the memories I left? Are the relationships I have a representation of who I am?"

When I answered these two questions, three things stood out. As a family member, I did not celebrate others in my family enough. Yes, they all knew I loved them, but some had not heard what they meant to me from my lips. The other thing that stood out was I had, for the most part, brought good to others, but I had one relationship where I held a grudge. Finally, I needed to forgive myself in the areas where I held onto guilt and judgment.

Reflecting on these relationships was such a gift. I would not have made it a point to think about my image in the world, how I was seen by others, or if it was how I wanted to be seen at any other time. I got to work. I called friends and family. I made sure I communicated my feelings for them. I celebrated each interaction. I also started a new tradition. When friends and loved ones are celebrating a birthday, I make it a point to speak words of praise and list the qualities they bring to the world. I lift them up with how important they are in my life and the lives of others. This new practice has brought a lot of joy and celebration to our family and has caught on—others also do it now.

I felt one relationship needed a reset. I worked on forgiveness for a few months. I sent this person (I'll call them Chris) love daily, at least three times per day. I also looked for opportunities to be around Chris to repattern my resentment. Prior to the illness, I avoided Chris because I felt constrictive energy in their presence. Now in Chris's presence, I praised them and listened to them from a different perspective, not as if they were someone who hurt me, but as the soul in front of me in the present moment. This new perspective allowed me to see their vulnerability, hurt, and the child inside that yearned for love. My resentment started to melt as I discovered the parts of them I had not connected to before. The person I saw now was different from the one I knew before.

I discovered Chris was oblivious to the hurt I felt. They had no recollection of the incident. The incident had played out in my head repeatedly for many years, and I built a shell of resentment around it. Repatterning that thought took time and practice. I had made the entire situation about me, and in the process, I became a prisoner to the memory. It took some months to work this out internally. Then one day Chris called me unexpectedly. The first thing I noticed was that my body was no longer contractive; it was expansive and I enjoyed my time talking with them. I felt differently about Chris. I enjoyed our conversation, feeling no judgment or ill emotions. This was a day of celebration. I felt free. I felt renewed and praised myself for transforming the relationship.

The interesting part of this process was that Chris has no idea I held a grudge all that time. Our relationship had not been close for many years because I was guarded, and Chris could feel it. Chris would apologize to me at times for no reason other than feeling they were intruding in my space. I could tell they felt judged and uncomfortable, but once I released the negative feelings about the situation, our relationship opened to a different level. Chris also felt free in our conversation. The energy opened, and now we have a different relationship, a supportive and loving one.

The other decision I made about forgiveness was to see the good in everyone no matter what. In the past, judgment of others could be my go-to emotion. If from my perspective the person was not being their best self, I judged them in my mind, thinking they could do better. I did not like that about myself; furthermore, as a life coach, I knew better. To change that, I made it a practice to catch my thoughts in those situations and repattern them by looking for the good in the person. Instead of judging them, I praised them in my head. It did not matter what it looked like on the outside, or the conversation or the situation; I looked for their good actions.

The opportunity to work on forgiveness daily is one reason I tell people I would not wish this journey on anyone, but I wish what I learned on everyone. Forgiveness is such a powerful tool. It transforms in unbelievable ways, and its beauty lies in being able to practice it without engaging the other party. It takes only one person to transform a relationship.

Law of Sacrifice

This law is about giving up something for a greater life. My example was in forgiveness since I gave up my resentment and judgment for the greater emotion of love. The sacrifice was in the practice, the discipline required to do the work. I practiced noticing when I was thinking of judgmental and blaming thoughts; then I had the discipline to replace those thoughts with love, praise, support, compassion, and kindness. It was not easy, and over time, honestly, I did not know whether it was working, but I kept at it, expecting and believing that my willingness and discipline to see differently would reflect in the way I saw them. As the Law of Sacrifice calls for having the discipline to change my thought processes, I welcomed a new perspective about the people and my relationship with them.

The Law of Sacrifice was also present in the diligence and commitment to feed my body health-supporting/restoring foods, so my discipline was making bone broth every Wednesday, taking my supplements daily, and walking even when I did not feel like it. The Law of Sacrifice works hand in hand with the mental faculty of will—you will yourself to do the things necessary for the higher good it will bring to you.

You have probably worked with the Law of Sacrifice without knowing it at times—every time you gave up something and substituted it with a discipline that you initially may not have felt excited about, but you did it anyway because of the results it would provide. It works the same in health, giving up the thoughts and feelings of "Why me?" or any thought that feeds your current situation without taking action to make it better. When you challenge yourself to see the illness differently, stop seeing it as an overwhelming thing that controls you, and start realizing you control how you feel, you are sacrificing sympathy to become the victor.

Law of Obedience

The Law of Obedience is about knowing you are not in charge and a being greater than you is working for the highest good of all concerned. It is understanding that what you experience today in the illness is for the greater good; therefore, obey it and follow where it leads. This law teaches being in harmony with the one God, the Universe, living in a state of trust that you are always in the right place without resistance.

This law is about listening to your inner guidance and living from the energy of love. This process challenges you to see where more practice in the laws is needed and to work on your perceptions. For instance, the normal reaction is to fear the disease, thus losing control of the self and believing in the disease instead of your Higher Power. When you are aligned with the power within, you listen to the small voice that guides you in caring for yourself. It empowers you to take steps to make your journey easy and flowing.

The Law of Obedience challenges you to be in harmony with God. It calls for you to stay connected to your inner guidance and listen to it no matter how uncomfortable it may be. You are uncomfortable in new situations, and the paradigms work to keep you stuck in what's familiar. But when you are stuck, you are not growing.

Growing is uncomfortable, and it requires remaining open to what life brings. You may not always like it, but trust that it is a gift for your highest good. Staying obedient to the life that unfolds calls for forever changing within. You are always evolving into a new self, a new being, and just when you uncover this new self, you see a call to step into another new being. Being obedient is about sharpening your tools to continue your spiritual growth.

The challenge I faced as I practiced following the Law of Obedience was that in our humanness, we think we are in control. We live our life following our five senses, so submitting to living differently was a challenge at first. I now believe that part of being on the cancer journey was about learning how the laws work. I was given the perfect experience to experiment and see results in my recovery in the most incredible way.

Obeying is submitting to what is offered. I submitted, I learned, I suffered, but most of all, I am now thriving. The journey was bumpy because of my humanness and tendencies to want to do things my way, yet when I "experimented" and submitted to the gift, it was a spiritual journey that opened my awareness to a new way of being. A Chinese Proverb says, "To get through the hardest journey we need take one step at a time, but we must keep on stepping."

Law of Success

This law is about how we are all equipped with the same faculties and opportunities. We must do the work to discover we create our own success and failure as it manifests in the way we approach a situation. When we approach situations from the perspective that we are healthy, vibrant, and expect good results, our reality rises to the expectation. God's intention for everyone is that we succeed, flourish, and prosper, so as we step into our vision of what we expect and see happening through us, everything around us conspires to provide that reality. Success comes when we trust the process and lean into life with a burning desire to succeed and knowing that "we can." We have no doubt we will obtain our goal because we've decided to do all we can do to make it happen.

From the time I opted for health, I had no doubt it was going to be the result of my health journey. As I write this, I still have work to do in this area, like maintaining the thought that the disease will not come back. It is common for cancer survivors to think of having to do it all over again. This is one reason I call myself a cancer thriver. I did not survive breast cancer; I am thriving in life as I move forward because I left cancer behind.

Success happens when you do two things well. You use your time and thoughts to work toward what you want. The thoughts I thought and the things I did were to reach my end goal of health. I used the other laws to reinforce the framework of thought and time. It was no different than when I set my mind to graduating from college, creating success in my vocation, or being part of a happy marriage. It required working on my thoughts and my time. When I did not make the investment of time and thought, then my results reflected my lack of dedication to my goal.

When we are thriving, the tendency is to get on an upward spiral that can become a self-fulfilling prophecy, leading us higher and higher. Redoubling our efforts to remain positive and continue our practices is key to staying on track in the journey. When I saw my energy depleting, it reflected disempowering thoughts I allowed to dwell inside me, so I discovered quickly that my thoughts were the tools to keep me on track. By aligning my thoughts with health, and allowing nothing other than health to be part of my journey it was simpler to stay on course and develop momentum.

Exercise

Consider each law and examine how it applies to you and the actions needed to activate and be in harmony with that law.

- Thinking—Pay attention to what you are thinking, remembering that everything is created twice. Your thoughts have the power of creation, so create the situation you would love. The condition or circumstance has no power. The power lives in you.

- Supply—We live in an abundant world. Lack is created in our mind, so living from a state of "I am healthy, vibrant, energetic, and loving life" is key because it shifts our focus to all the good we have in our life. When we focus on the illness, more of the symptoms and side effects will be displayed. Focus instead on the supply of love and care you are receiving from the medical community, family, and friends.

- Attraction—Pay attention to what you are paying attention to. The focus of your attention is what you are attracting into your life, so concentrate on health, praise, and love. You have a burning desire and expectation of health and wellness; therefore, focus on being grateful for life, for the health you currently have, and for all the wellness wishes you are given. Every sentiment of wellness is placed in your bank toward receiving the health you deserve.

- Receiving—Are you a giver or a receiver by nature? Remember, you have to give to activate the Law of Receiving. If you desire health, act as if you had the health you desire. Embrace a routine you would use if you were healthy—gardening, dates with loved ones, and attending events. It may be difficult to show up, but remember, in showing up, you are embracing life, and ultimately, that is what you want. Give your body the love and nutrients to help it receive the health you are expecting.

- Increase—Are you cursing the disease and how it has affected your life? If that is the case, then adopt an attitude of praise for the good in your life, the good things that have come about because of the illness. Praise your body for the work it is doing. Love yourself for staying in tune with life. When you praise, you raise the vibration for yourself and others. Making praise a part of your life sets a mood of happiness that is infectious and leads to a focus on wellness and gratitude.

- Compensation—What seeds are you planting? They will grow as compensation for your efforts. Are you making efforts to get well, or are you dwelling in the illness? The fruits of your labor will be what you put forth, so you must step out of the condition and step into health with your thoughts, feelings, and actions.

- Non-Resistance—If you are resisting the life, the treatments, and the illness, then you are living in struggle. You are adding friction to your situations, and when you submit to non-resistance, the flow and ease of life will appear. That does not mean succumb to the disease. It means you accept what is and continue to move toward health. Stop the struggle because it will delay your recovery. Acceptance means you are no longer in fear, and your body has the opportunity to heal.

- Forgiveness—Are you holding on to emotions that are depleting you? Do you feel resentment, anger, shame, judgment, guilt, apathy, and blame? These energies are not serving your recovery. Transforming your perception of what happened to transform those feelings is work worth doing in support of healing and recovery.

- Sacrifice—Which things in your health journey are no longer serving you? Which of the laws above require repatterning? In the repatterning of old habits, you will need the discipline to do the work and change the flow from contractive to expansive. If the issue is your thinking, then start noticing what you notice about your thoughts and stay disciplined in the practice of generating life-giving thoughts. To get the results you want, give up (sacrifice) the old patterns and adopt new ways of doing, thinking, and feeling.

Decide to do the work, taking a step daily, and making progress as you build the cadence and momentum to work and repattern that part of your life.

Recommendation: Be kind to yourself. Start with one or two changes so the flow of energy stays focused on attaining the desired goal. Once you feel you have traction, move to other areas. It takes rigor to continue doing the work, so it is helpful to set daily reminders and/or follow constructive, positive routines throughout your day.

Summary

Working with these eleven truth principles, known as "The Law" is a way of life. Remain consistent in the work with the attitude of *No matter what is happening around me, I am staying true to this practice, and I am not surprised by it but continue to be amazed by how it works all the time.* Like any law, like the Law of Gravity or Velocity, this Law is real. It provides an awakening to the work that must continue daily—we get no days off from thinking expansively. The fleeting thoughts of "hatred toward my body image" turned into a thing. That is real. Stephen Covey said, "Every human being has four endowments—self-awareness, conscience, independent will and creative imagination. These give us the ultimate human freedom." Remaining aware of what we think, what we feel, and how we act takes a lifetime of work, discipline, and consistency. I am a student of this awakening. While it is a daily practice, some days are good and others are not. That is how I successfully walked with breast cancer and now walk with life.

A Chinese proverb said, "A journey of a thousand miles begins with a single step." I remind myself that when I am in the present, I only have one step to take. In your human journey, let the step be consistent with walking with "The Law." I do not claim it is easy, but it is in the effort that you will tap into your soul to heal your body, mind, and spirit and magically grow.

A Final Note

Now what? Now that you've read and finished my book, are you doing some of the suggested exercises and practices? Are you setting goals for yourself knowing anything is possible, and you just have to decide to make it happen? What other books are you reading or webinars are you attending? Have you set an intention to change and taken steps to make it happen?

I challenge you to act! While you may have been inspired to act by this book, you may not have not done so yet. Like Mahatma Gandhi said, "The future depends on what you do today." What you focus on today bears the fruit of what will be tomorrow, so there is no better time than the present to act. There are no coincidences. When you decided to buy this book, part of you was seeking growth. Now you just have to do the work, take action, and apply the material daily. On the lines below, list seven to ten action steps you are willing to commit to taking in the next ninety days. There is magic in creating the results you love by committing to defined practices for ninety days. I promise you will discover a new way of being.

_____

_____

_____

_____

_____

_____

_____

_____

_____

In this book, you learned life has a rhythm. You learned offering less resistance to life was more effective and efficient. Invisible laws and mental faculties you may not have been using prior to reading this book now allow you to live from a different level of awareness. Your perspective about the circumstances in your life has changed. You can neutralize the conditions of the outside world by not calling them good or bad, but merely staying curious about the gift you will receive from the experience.

If you apply the knowledge, learn from the experiences, develop your skills, and use the techniques and strategies herein, which you are invited to make your own, then you will be living a genius life and tapping into your soul to heal your body, mind, and spirit. I do not claim it will be easy, but I know it does become part of who you are, and it becomes easy when you become the person you are meant to be.

Having read this book and experimented with the exercises, I encourage you to contact me and tell me about "the good, the bad, and the ugly" of your experience with this book. My goal is to improve it on each printing so more people can benefit.

More importantly, I would love to hear about you, your challenges, your obstacles, your intentions, and your dreams. I would love to help you. In fact, you are invited to a complimentary *discovery session*, which is a one-hour consultation with me by phone or Zoom. Much of the magic happens in moments of discovery.

My email address is edna@livingrealitydreams.com, and my cell is (925) 202-1042, so please email or text me with your name and time zone, so we can schedule your complimentary consultation.

I hold for you the thought that your highest aspirations, the healing of your mind, body, and spirit, lead to the discovery of how your life is a gift for everyone connected to you. You are a luminous spiritual being, living a human journey that brings you back to Self. Enjoy the journey!

Your friend,

About the Author

EDNA A. CASTILLO is an internationally known author, inspirational professional keynote speaker, life coach, and breast cancer thriver. She has a bachelor's degree in business and became a successful business leader in her industry while discovering her coaching gift and desire to serve. She is a Certified Transformational Life Coach by the Brave Thinking Institute and has been studying and practicing success life principles for more than twenty years. As the founder of RealityDreams Life Coaching, LLC, Edna loves supporting others to live into their dreams and wellness by developing their inner genius and living a life of purpose and love.

In 2020, Edna was diagnosed with breast cancer. Thriving on what she turned into a spiritual journey, she was not only healed but released into a discovery of miracles and nuggets of wisdom that she now shares with others. Edna believes her breast cancer was an offering from God to better serve her clients. Her burning desire to help others navigate a rigorous health condition was birthed from her own experience.

Edna has also been called to coach women whose cultural paradigms get in the way of them fulfilling their purposes and love for life. She has overcome her own self-limiting beliefs from her religious and cultural background so she can fulfill her God-given purpose.

As the author of *Living Your Intuitive Genius*, Edna helps each client tap into their soul to heal their body, mind, and spirit. Her love for people and life itself is her "why" and the reason she steps outside her comfort zone as an introvert to do the thing she loves most—help others discover the power within to do what they would love to do, to be, to have, to give, and to create.

Edna was born in Guatemala, but since age ten, she has adopted the San Francisco Bay Area as home, giving her a rich bicultural experience. She still lives by The Bay with her husband, Daniel. She loves to cook for family and friends, enjoys walking or hiking in nature, and delights in quiet time in the redwoods near the coast where she communes with nature and welcomes new ideas, dreams, and inspiration.

Hire Edna A. Castillo to Speak at Your Next Event

When it comes to choosing a professional speaker for your next event, you will find no one more respected or successful and uniquely qualified than Edna A. Castillo. Edna's experience as a Certified Transformational Life Coach and public speaker results from more than thirty years of studying and living the tenets she shares with her audience.

Edna brings absolute passion to her professional speaking events as she inspires both healthy audiences and those battling cancer and other health diagnoses. Her personal relationship with cancer and wellness aroused in her a motivational approach that will leave your audience or colleagues with a renewed love for life.

As a Cancer Thriver, Edna delivers healing and wellness presentations to healing and support communities across the world. Whether your audience is 10 or 10,000, in person or virtual, Edna will convey a customized message of inspiration for your meeting or conference. She understands your audience's desire to hear from someone who lives their message while instilling hope and knowledge about the real-life situations they are living. Edna offers many nuggets of wisdom and hope, but her favorite is how in our toughest moments, the seeds of greatness are birthed to create richer, fuller lives.

Edna's bicultural background and life experience fuels her appetite to deliver her message to both English and Spanish-speaking audiences. As a woman who overcame cultural limiting paradigms, she shares a liberating message to empower women into their greatness. She has a unique understanding of how disease can be perceived in Hispanic communities, which adds to her message's power and impact.

Overall, Edna's speaking philosophy is to entertain, inspire, and impart the confidence of healing so people can achieve extraordinary results. If you are looking for a memorable speaker who will leave your audience wanting more, book Edna A. Castillo today!

To receive a highlight video of Edna and find out whether she is available for your next meeting, visit her site at the address below. Then contact her by phone or email to schedule a complimentary pre-speech phone interview.

www.LivingRealityDreams.com

edna@livingrealitydreams.com

(925) 202-1042

Experience the Life-Changing Magic of Edna A. Castillo's Coaching

Since Edna A. Castillo listened to her intuitive genius to follow her calling in life coaching, she has never looked back. As a Certified Transformational Life Coach and Life Mastery Consultant with the Brave Thinking Institute, she founded RealityDreams Life Coaching LLC. She serves women who are journeying through a tough diagnosis or simply wanting to grow into the next level of their own Becoming.

Edna's evocative style of coaching takes many forms, depending on the client and the results they seek. Edna coaches group and one-on-one clients in various programs, including DreamBuilder, Life Mastery, Working with the Law, Into Your Genius, or her own programs of Healing and Wellness. As her client, you are invited to invest in your growth to heal your body, mind, and spirit to live the life you deserve and love.

If you are open to hearing from your intuitive genius to create healing, growth, and prosperity in every area of your life, consider joining one of her inspired programs:

1. Living Your RealityDreams Group and One-on-One—weekly study and Q&A

2. VIP Coaching, Masterminds, and Supports

3. Classes, Workshops, Retreats, Podcasts, and Blogs

4. Resources and Healing and Wellness Strategies

5. E-Books

Learn about customized packages for Life Coaching; Living in Wellness; Healing your Body, Mind, and Soul; Living Your Intuitive Genius, Stepping into Your Becoming; The Thriver's Journey; and more much more.

To discuss further how Edna can help you live your intuitive genius, contact her at:

www.LivingRealityDreams.com

edna@livingrealitydreams.com

(925) 202-1042